Pathways to Healing: A 60 Day Empowerment Devotional for Survivors of Sexual Abuse

KIMBERLY R. MAYES, MSW

Pathways to Healing: A 60 Day Empowerment Devotional for Survivors of Sexual Abuse

By Kimberly Mayes

Copyright © 2014 by Kimberly R. Mayes

She is Me Publications, Silver Spring, Maryland

All rights reserved. No part of this publication may be reproduced or transmitted in any form or by any means, electronic or mechanical, including photocopying and recording, or introduced into any information storage and retrieval system without the written permission of the copyright owner and the publisher of this book. Brief quotations may be used in reviews prepared for inclusion in a magazine, newspaper or for broadcast. For further information please contact:

She Is Me Publications
8705B Colesville Rd, Ste B #174
Silver Spring, MD 20910

ISBN 13: 978-0-9909055-0-9
ISBN 10: 0990905500

Printed in the United States of America

FIRST EDITION

All scripture quotations, unless otherwise indicated, are taken from THE HOLY BIBLE, NEW LIVING TRANSLATION. © 1996, Used by permission of Tyndale House Publishers, Inc. Wheaton, IL 60189. All rights reserved.
Scripture quotations noted NIV are taken from THE HOLY BIBLE, NEW INTERNATIONAL VERSION®, NIV®, © 1973, 1978, 1984, by International Bible Society. Used by permission of Zondervan. All rights reserved.
Scripture quotations noted ESV are taken from THE HOLY BIBLE, ENGLISH STANDARD VERSION®, ESV®, © 2001 by Crossway, a publishing ministry of Good News Publishers. All rights reserved.
Scripture quotations noted GW are taken from THE HOLY BIBLE, GOD'S WORD®, ©1995 God's Word to the Nations. Used by permission of Baker Publishing Group.
Scripture quotations noted KJV are taken from the King James Version of the Bible.

Cover Design: Sony Laventure
Editors: Caleine Ajusma & Dawn Swayne
Hair: Hair By Newg
Make-Up Artist: Makeup By Don
Photographer: Stevenson Charlot
Stylist: Tia Speed

DEDICATION

This is dedicated to every woman who has spent her nights
in tears and her days in silence because of sexual abuse.
May the God of peace and restoration LIVE in your soul.
To my Uncle Chris, your smiles and joy will forever live in my soul.

CONTENTS

	Acknowledgments	i
	Introduction	ii
1	Fear	1
2	Strength	15
3	Purpose	29
4	Faith	43
5	Trust & Forgiveness	57
6	Restoration	71
7	Beauty	85
8	Love & Relationships	99
9	Grace	113

ACKNOWLEDGMENTS

I would like to thank God for His unconditional love and strength that has rained down on me on my personal *Pathways to Healing*. I am honored to have You in my life and would be nothing without You.

To my mother, may you live in freedom, peace and joy as God radiates in your heart.

To all of my sisters who have cried, laughed, prayed and listened to my infinite days and nights of hurt and confusion, I love you. God placed you in my life at strategic times to push me through each rough moment, and you took on my weight! Thank you.

To Caleine Ajusma and Dawn Swayne, thank you for your spirit filled editing, you have made this message pristine.

To Sheri Hairston, I have never met a spirit so angelic in human form. Thank you for encouraging me to continue to write at the beginning of this process. God used you to make me see the worth of every single word that will be read in the forthcoming pages.

To my Pastor Roderick Hairston, the simplicity of your encouraging words and sermons spoke to the very core of who I am in Christ. It is through you I believed in the God in me.

To my celebrity mentors, Iyanla Vanzant, thank you for confirming that my passion is what drives change and I can live in freedom. To Tyrese Gibson, you spoke to me with every video posted on Facebook. During this writing process, God used you to empower me to become who He needs me to be for hurting women, thank you. To TD Jakes, your messages brought revelation to my life to be a steward over what God has trusted me with, His people. Thank you for your dedication to ministry.

To anyone I have ever introduced myself to, may you understand my truth and passion for life as you read my story of healing.

To myself, you are beautiful…..

INTRODUCTION
KIMBERLY R. MAYES, MSW

This devotional was birthed about out of despair. I travel home to Miami, FL often, and I always take the opportunity to read the Word and pray to my Father on the beach, as the sun is rising. January 2, 2014, I was on the beach at 5am, crying. Crying and asking God to make my life have purpose and meaning. To my knowledge, there was nothing that brought me to the feeling of such despair, I was enjoying life! In this moment, there was such a burden to ask Him for a clear answer of His next steps in my life.

God revealed to me in 2010 my purpose, to walk along side women on their journey to freedom from sexual abuse, but there was something more He needed from me. As the sun began to rise, He told me to start writing. God speaks to me through nature often, so I began to look at His glory rising before me for inspiration. I began to feel the wind of His peace as I looked at the shoreline, birds were lined-up along the beach marveling at His glory too! I captured the moment because I could not believe my eyes. I began to run my feet through the sand and He had me to look at all of the seashells on the shore, that was the beginning of this devotional and the moment He gave me the poem *Seashells*. As I began to write, God expressed to me the pain I was feeling for so many years as a survivor of sexual abuse should be written down. So many emotions were rushing through my mind and body at the mere thought of writing down 20 years of pain and growth. I had no idea that moment of emptiness would bring about such beauty in the pages you are about to read.

I had rough days while in the writing process. I felt the pain and even saw some of the very real situations you went through. While writing down the years of growing pains and mistakes, some feelings of regret and anger came back, but God reminded me of His grace, love, and mercy as I began to re-read the God breathed material He gave me to deliver to you.

Understand there will some good days and there will be some bad days as you journey through *Pathways to Healing*, but always remember, God is there. My writing style is a bit unique, but it is in the format that God wanted me to speak to you in, poetry. I believe with this unique perspective, God will grace you with bold truths and free you of the false realities existing in your mind.

Each week you will journey through a topic that most of us have faced on our *Pathways to Healing*, to ensure there is freedom and peace to move forward in life. You will also have quiet time to fast and pray to God about each weeks topic (Matthew 17:21). This will be the most important time of the week for you because you will have the opportunity to hear from God about how He wants to heal you specifically. There are several ways you can fast, a specific time period (i.e. 6am-12pm), sun up to sun down, or a meal (i.e.

breakfast, lunch, dinner). There are also several ways that you can fast in regards to food and daily pleasures that can be a distraction from hearing God. For instance, a complete fast (i.e. no food, only water), the Daniel Fast, turning off the TV and giving up your social media accounts for the timeframe of your fast. You can fast however the Spirit leads you, but please be mindful that a fast is to bring clarity to your mind and authority over your flesh, be prayerful about your specific sacrifice to God. Also, if you have a medical condition that prevents you from fasting food, please be in prayer about the things that are a sacrifice to you.

I won't take it for granted that everyone who will be journeying through this devotional has accepted Jesus Christ as their Lord and Savior. If you have not, please take a moment to recite this simple prayer to ensure that your salvation is secure and your healing under the blood of Jesus will be powerful beyond measure:

> "Lord, I am a sinner (Romans 3:23) and I ask You to forgive me of my sins as I turn to You (Romans 6:23). Heavenly Father, I believe in my heart that Jesus lived and died for my sins and He rose from the dead (Romans 10:9) so that I may live in freedom (Romans 8:1). I ask that You fill me with the Holy Spirit. I thank You for coming into my heart so I may live according to Your Word and in eternity with You (Romans 10:10, 13). I thank You for my renewed mind and spirit as I am a new creation in You (2 Corinthians 5:17). Dwell in me and give me wisdom to live a sound and prosperous life until I am called home to be with You. In Jesus' name, Amen!"

You are on a *Pathways to Healing* my sister. A pathway that will be a winding road and seem as though it will never end. When you reach the point of your destination, you will feel whole and free. God already began a new work in you, if you don't think so, just reflect on the day you bought this devotional. He already began the work because you have the courage to tap into a place of healing. As survivors, the first step to healing is the hardest because we don't know what it will look like to be free and exposed, but you took the first step. You took the first step with the hope that you will be refreshed and renewed. I am proud of you!

As you journey through this devotional, please tell someone you trust about your choice to walk in freedom, don't walk through this alone! Also, get connected with someone in your pastoral care ministry at your church and/or a reputable therapist in your community. My prayer for you as you journey through the *Pathways to Healing*, God uses this devotional to bring you closer to Him like never before. Happy healing!

FEAR

HEAR ME

Lord, hear my cry.
Please, please, Lord.
Please, Lord.

I'm afraid and I never thought it would be this way,
I'm looking forward to the day
That I will be set free, from this misery.

Please, please Lord.
Please, do it for me.

Keep me
Free me
Move me.
Keep me
Free me
Move me.

Please, please Lord.
Please, Lord, please.

You're praying to Me out of fear.
Your spirit is not here with Me....It's caught up in yesterday.
You do know that My Son died for you, so that you may live
Even in your despair.

Honey, raise your eyes to Me.
I gave you victory.
You may not understand the evils of this world,
But I challenge you to give Me your hand.

To
Keep you.
Free you.
Move you.

I Am your refuge.
I Am your peace.
I Am your key to freedom.
I Am the gravity that keeps you grounded when you want to fall,
Yet you smile and stay standing.

Trust Me.
Believe Me.
Seek Me.

I Am your freedom.
Let there be no fear in your heart,
For I have already given you freedom, My love.

Scripture

2 Corinthians 3:17 (NIV)

"Now the Lord is the Spirit, and where the Spirit of the Lord is, there is freedom."

Reflection

As women who are overcomers of sexual abuse, we tend to take on the spirit of fear because our troubles and pain are so real to us. We cower and get lost in the pain that is so common and routine that we forget who we are and WHOSE we are. God never intended for sexual abuse to be a weapon against us, but the enemy tries to use it as such. As you continue on your journey to freedom and healing, remember, God wants you to keep your eyes on Him as you walk daily in this life. You are more than a conquer and will live in freedom!

Prayer

God, as we pray to You, help us to calm our spirits and know that no matter the size of the gaping hole in our hearts or the magnitude of fear that we feel, You are always there. Help us to remember the sacrifice that You took for us and help us to feel the love of Christ. I plead the blood of Jesus over Your daughter and come against the spirit of fear and anxiety, for with You, we can confidently walk in the freedom that You established for us so long ago. Thank You, its in Your Son's name we pray.

Amen!

KEEP WALKING

Time reveals my mess and my flaws,
But You are the Master and Deliverer of all.

I choose to abide and live in You,
To be consumed and transformed,
By the wonderful miracles You do.

Sometimes I think to myself,
Who, what and where did You go?
But in my earnest prayers,
I am always reminded.

No matter how much I hurt,
You say, "Come to Me."

No matter how bad my past looks,
You say, "Come to Me."

No matter how dim my future looks,
You say, "Come to Me."

You see, You show all of the wonderful truths,
Of what it means to love unconditionally.
I don't know what it looks like on the other side,
But I know that You will always be with me.

Scripture

Psalm 145:18 (NIV)

"The Lord is near to all who call on him, to all who call on him in truth."

Reflection

Confusion. Uncertainty. Judgment. Fear. And so much more happens when we begin to walk towards healing. It can be scary! Who wants to hear about the dark secrets of sexual abuse? I know one person who does, Jesus. There is comfort in knowing that our biggest cheerleader is standing at the finish line, cheering us on to run towards Him. Don't look left, and don't look right, keep running towards Him! When your past begins to look like its catching up to you, cry out to Him and let Him know you need help. He will give you the wind you need to push you across the finish line!

Prayer

Father, sometimes my days get so heavy. And I think about the embarrassment that I have gone through, and it just seems too much to bear. Thank You for Your healing grace and for Your Word that covers all that has ever happened. Show me how to move my legs as I sometimes tremble in fear as I am walking towards You. Bind up my past as Satan tries to use it as a means to deter me from walking towards You. Loose my peace and destiny in You. I love You and trust You with all that I am, in Jesus' name.

Amen!

I DIDN'T KNOW

I look to You,
For healing and strength.
I look to You,
To take away the misery.
I look to You,
To make me whole again.
I look to You,
To give me freedom from my past.
I look to You,
To make the tormenting stop.
I look to You,
To make my days brighter.
I look to You,
To give me a new life.
I look to You,
For my next blessing.

          All the while
          I have forgotten
          I am saved.

I am Your daughter,
The Holy Sprit lives in me.
That same Spirit gives me the authority
To demand that I be
Healed and strengthened.
Free from pain
Whole in Christ's name.
Free from my past
With no one tormenting me.
Living brighter days
Renewed in my mind
To receive my next blessing.
I didn't know
You trusted me so much.
With Holy Spirit living in me
I choose to be free.
Free from the tactics of the enemy.

Scripture

Romans 8:11 (NLT)

"The Spirit of God, who raised Jesus from the dead, lives in you. And just as God raised Christ from the dead, He will give life to your mortal bodies by the same spirit living within you."

Reflection

How many times have you chosen to live in fear and plead with God to make your life right? How many times have you said, "If You will just, (fill in the blank), I will be ok!"? As Christ followers, we as survivors tend to forget the power that lives within us. The power of the Holy Spirit, who desires to live at His highest peak within us, is waiting to live through you. The Holy Spirit Empowers (Acts 1:8), Directs (Acts 8:29), Defends (Isaiah 59:19), Comforts (Acts 9:31), Gives Freedom (Romans 8:2), Guides (Ezekiel 36:27), Gives Joy (1 Thessalonians 1:6), Loves (Romans 5:5), Mentors (John 14:16), Renews (Titus 3:5), Gives Strength (Psalms 51:12) and He does so much more! Never forget the power of the Holy Spirit that lives in you. Activate His power through prayer and worship!

Prayer

Father, in the name of Jesus, forgive me for overlooking Your glory of the Holy Spirit that resides in me as a firm believer in Your Word. Help me to discover Your Spirit more as I walk along this *Pathways to Healing*. Thank You for choosing me to live a life of power and strength through the Holy Spirit. I love You and thank You for blessing me with the power to be an overcomer and thrive in Your Kingdom. In Jesus' name.

Amen!

CREEPY

I see you
Lurking in the corner
Waiting to devour me
Like a tiger
Ready to hunt his prey.

I vowed never to see another person like you
Keeping far way
Forever and a day.

Never to be preyed on again.

I see so many like you
Whenever I pass downtown
Men, lurking and waiting
To devour their next prey.
Only they are looking for their next hit
Of the chemical that takes them to another world.

You on the other hand
Abused me just the same,
You couldn't live without me.

My God!

Protect me from the lurks
And preys of men alike.

Scripture

Psalm 91:4 (NLT)

"He will cover you with feathers. He will shelter you with his wings. His faithful promises are your armor and protection."

Reflection

Fear swells up in us everyday, to keep us in bondage and away from happy and rational things. There were so many times that I saw drug addicts walking the streets and I would be disgusted and in fear of what they could do to me. My abuser was an addict, so similarities struck a chord with me. This was not an unreasonable fear. I needed to make sure I was alert but often times I would cringe in such fear that my behavior changed and I would be extremely irrational in my thinking. This fear controlled me in a way where I could not function. To allow the sight of someone else to keep me standing in fear is just what the enemy wanted. God is a Healer and a He is a Mind Regulator. As you think about the people and things that cause you to cower in fear, write them down and bring them before God as we pray.

Prayer

Lord, my sister needs You. She needs You to restore her happiness and remove her fears. God, the list of fears that she brings before You are real to her and I am asking that You free her from these fears so she is no longer held in bondage of remembering her abuse every turn she makes. I honor You for Your healing and for Your peace that You are giving my sister. Right now in the name of Jesus please replace her fears with joy, peace, love and a hedge of protection to feel safe and free in You. I love You and I trust my sister is now at peace. In Jesus' name.

Amen!

SILLY GIRL

Heart racing.
Stomach rumbling.
I can't believe I am tumbling
Down to my knees in such agony.
Headaches and pain
My face, curled in disdain
Just thinking about the outpour of rain
On my life.
I cry, I ask for help
"Lord, please give me ...."
I can't even pray.
I call my girlfriend and say
"I need your help, I can't seem to think."
                                        "What's wrong? Is everything ok?"
"No, I need you to pray."
We pray and I feel a shift.
                                   "It's the enemy making you feel like this."
I hear God speak.

I don't care what it is
Know that I am the God of peace.
Money, food, car, job, clothes
None of those things will ever amount to
The gold streets paved in My home.
So the pain, worry and fear you see
Will not add one day to your life
So let Me be the One who moves your mountains.
Satan will try to trick you
Always remember,
He will give you strife
That is his job you see.
Recall, My Son died
So you can
Have life more abundantly.
So stand tall
And let Me hear you speak.
I want to hear your voice daughter
It sounds so sweet.
What has your heart racing?
Turn it over to ME.

Scripture

1 Peter 5:7 (NLT)

"Cast your worries and cares to God, for he cares about you."

Reflection

Money, food and gas. Those were the 3 things that Satan played up in my life. I would be so scared to look at my bank account some days. I would stock pile on food, I was always worried that I would never have enough. Why was this such a factor in my life? The day I wrote this devotional was the day after an incident where I was scared out of my mind about being able to survive until my next paycheck. But He reminded me, your dependence of survival is on the 3 big essentials in a person life, money, food and gas for your car, not Me. Satan knew that my dependence was in those "things" instead of the Creator of ALL things! Silly me huh? This is a real and "legitimate' situation because life can be rough without them, but the only thing I know that is more life changing than money, food and gas is God the Father. What areas has Satan magnified in your life that have been causing you to live in fear? Write them down as we go before our Father.

Prayer

God You said in Your Word that You shall supply ALL of our needs and I am asking You to rain down peace, clarity and deliverance of dependence on natural things and people upon my sister right now. Satan has held her hostage long enough and we are asking for Your comfort to replace that place of fear and Your hedge of protection to guard my sister's heart and mind. She loves You dearly and I am asking that You fill every need in her life so she never cowers in fear to Satan ever again! In Jesus' name.

Amen!

FEAR ACTIVITY

The number one area we struggle with as survivors is fear. The enemy chooses to use this very real and frightful tactic to keep us bound and timid to move forward in the freedom and the glory of God. I remember nights when I was afraid to close my eyes because I felt as though I would be reliving my reality as I tried to rest. As a survivor, fear of the most mundane thing can cripple us to possibly live a recluse life or simply in the shadows of others. I say no more!

In Psalm 118:6 (ESV) David clearly states, "The LORD is on my side; I will not fear. What can man do to me?" What can man do to you now that you have the Lord your God standing on your side? As you have journeyed through this chapter, find peace in knowing that nothing and no one can remove the shield of protection that is upon you.

FEAR ACTIVITY

As survivors we tend to have lofty and unrealistic thoughts, that are understandably warranted, but cause us to experience excessive anxiety and fear. Recognizing the true nature of a circumstance can eliminate the worrisome thoughts we experience.

For instance, I began to feel uneasy around men because my abuser was a male. When men were in my presence, I began to think of all of the negative possibilities that can occur without actually experiencing any negative encounters with that particular individual.

A way for one to counteract those negative and anxious thoughts is to look at all sides of a scenario. Below is one scenario with two possible outcomes, one positive and one negative, that can occur when fear evokes an emotion:

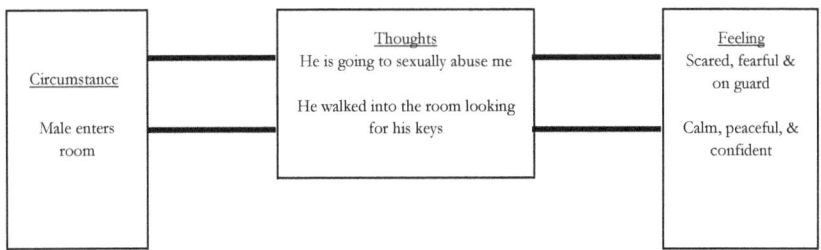

1. Having a traumatic past causes our memory to engage our fight or flight senses more often than normal as a means to prevent further harm. Therefore, identify the specific thoughts that cause your fight or flight senses to go in to overdrive.

2. Be realistic in your observation of thoughts. Because fear is based on the *possibility* of a dangerous or harmful situation occurring, it is safe to say our thoughts and feelings can be false at times.

3. *Completely* analyze why and how you are responding to a specific situation and ask yourself, "Are my thoughts and feelings about this particular situation valid?"

TIME WITH GOD

Your ability to recognize the dreaded fear you have been feeling over time, is simply smoke and mirrors, will allow you to press into another level of healing. Now that you have taken some time to analyze your thoughts and feelings, its time to pray and fast with God for guidance (please read page ii for fasting guidance). Take the time today to journal the rationale for your thoughts and feelings and bring them before God.

In your personal time with God:

1. Read Deuteronomy 31:6 to give you peace and understanding of your right not to be fearful.

2. Begin to pray and ask God to reveal places in which you are afraid and may have never noticed. Pray for the discernment to hear His instructions on navigating through moments of fear so you are able to peacefully move forward in grace and confidence.

3. Fast and meditate on your time spent with God today.

STRENGTH

CHECKMATE

I love you,
You're such a queen,
Always abounding in love and grace.
Most people think you were created
To simply be admired
With no direction
To be manipulated at the hands
Of the wisest player.
But the wisest is He
Playing His greatest opponent, Satan.
He moves you forward,
                                              Satan moves you right.

This game of life
Will certainly be a match.
The game is fixed
Little does Satan know
That you are the most powerful
Piece on the board.
He moves you forward,
                                              The Adversary moves you back,

And you fall.
God sees your pain
His plan is to rescue you
Satan has to be slain.
He moves you diagonal,
                                              The Deceiver moves you left.

I put my trust in Him
I will make it
I see the end in sight.
Just when I thought I had to use my might
He lifts me up
And places me down.
"Checkmate!" He yells, to his lowly opponent,
"My baby girl alwayswears the victor crown."

Scripture

Luke 10:18 (NLT)

"Yes" he told them, "I saw Satan fall from heaven like lightening."

Reflection

Satan does not like you. In fact I would go as far to say he hates you. You have his greatest opponent, God, guiding you with every move you make in life. Satan is so cleaver, he knows that if God is leading you, he has no chance of winning. You are powerful sis! You were created to be the greatest piece of ammunition that God has on His team. Remember your worth. Remember the game is already fixed, Satan has already been defeated! Nothing that anyone has done to you or anything you have done to yourself will change your value. You are powerful by nature, but you will only be useful in your power if you let God move you. Let Him use you!

Prayer

God, Your daughter is a powerful soul created to further Your Kingdom. She is standing alone and has fallen so many times to the hands of another and may have made the wrong moves in her life. She has seen herself on the loosing side, but God! You are so powerful and gracious that You can command claim of the board and take over. Lord, we give You all rights to 'our' lives and ask that You restore my sisters' soul to her rightful place, as a powerhouse who has been handcrafted diligently. Renew her mind and her view of herself Lord. Please, have her open her heart to entrust You to make all of the moves for her life. We love You and thank You in advance for the victory that we know is already won. In Jesus' name.

Amen!

BRICK WALLS

Walls, walls, walls,
They will eventually come crumbling down.
Walls, walls, walls,
Are built on all sides of town.

In good yards
And bad ones too.
I want them all to come down
So I can see straight through.
To your house
Where a gray cloud remains.
One day I'll come knocking
So I can tell you things have changed.
I'm a woman with purpose
And so much beauty.
You probably thought
I was too young to remember.
But lets not forget
I was the tender age of 5
And very much alive
To all the things you did to me.

Walls, walls, walls,
I told you they'll come down.
We are starting with one
Called the truth.
All too often it pained me to speak
But since I'm here
I'll tell it to you

You molested me.

Walls, walls, walls,
Fear just went running out the door.
All the walls of this house will fall.
No more will I stand with my mouth wide shut
For an eternity, nothing would come out.
But today, these walls will crumble
In pieces they will be.

Walls, walls, walls,
Expose this man,
For everything he did to me.

Scripture

Ephesians 5:13 (NLT)

"But their evil intentions will be exposed when the light shines on them."

Reflection

Have you thought about confronting your abuser? Have you considered the highs and lows of what it will be like for you to face the person who took so much away from you? I have and I felt such freedom. Freedom to be the strong woman I know I am. Before I felt freedom, I have to be honest, I felt fear, but it was the best thing I could have ever done. Think about the power you will gain back just speaking your truth. You won't only get power back but you will get your voice too. Something you probably have not heard in years or perhaps ever. My prayer for you is that you seek God about getting your voice back by confronting your abuser. Not in a spirit of violence but in a spirit of confidence and a spirit of healing. Whether through a simulated confrontation or an actual confrontation ask your Father what is the right way for YOU to get your voice back. Tinges of fear may be rising in you right now as you think about what may become of a confrontation, don't let that deter you from praying to your Father about His desires for your freedom.

Prayer

Lord, I'm asking that You whisper in Your daughter's ear Your will for her life in regards to confronting her abuser. Prepare her heart, her spirit, and her future for what is to come with confrontation, simulated or in person. Give her wisdom as she seeks wise counsel on any next steps You give her. Give her a glimpse of the freedom and peace that comes with standing on Your Word. In Jesus' Name.

Amen!

SILENCE

I cried on the inside
For weeks straight
I never knew I had so many tears.
So fragile
I prepared myself to break
Like an aged skeleton.
I began to keep up at night
Sleep was not my friend.
Walking around in silence
With no one to notice
My emotions living on my face.
Why can't I just tell someone?
I had a monster
Living in my home.
Conversations with people
Became too much
Silence is what always touched
My lips and mind.

But I say no more to you!
Yes you reading this!
You are my sister
Silence will kill you no more.

I speak life into that lifeless body.
I speak hope into the Spirit of your being.
I speak joy into your beautiful laughs.
I speak purpose into that wonderful dreams!

NO. MORE. SILENCE!
I refuse to hear
That you have been knocked down
By someone who doesn't care
About the life my Father created.

You my sister,
Will no longer be silent.
I am here with you
Let's pray together
As we ask the Lord to make your voice LOUD!

Scripture

Psalm 32:3 (NIV)

"When I kept my silent, my bones wasted away through my groaning all day."

Reflection

You will no longer be held down by someone who thought less of you. You will no longer be filled with empty dreams of what could have been. You will no longer keep your mouth sealed shut to give the enemy the win. You will no longer feel like what you have been through. NO MORE! I love you. I may never meet you a day in my life, but know that as these words are being written on this page, I hear you claiming the victory over your life. I don't know how old or how young you are but it is never too late for you to decree and declare the Lord's freedom over your life. Open your mouth and decree and declare, "I am no longer bound by the visions of my past." "I am no longer afraid to speak life into myself." "I am no longer tied to what others treated me as." "I am no longer defined by what was!"

Prayer

God, speak Your truth over Your daughter's life. Be the voice that she has not had for years. As my sister sleeps, whisper Your truth upon her life and begin to give her the confidence to have a voice to speak up about her abuse with wisdom. Thank You Lord for the voice that will be heard by her own ears for the very first time. I love You for my sister's life. In Jesus' name.

Amen!

D-DAY

No turning back.
A decision has been made
To wipe my tears away.

I'm moving on with life.
Never to forget
What made me strong.

Today and everyday here after
I declare trust in only You
To emancipate me.

I know it could only be You
And Your loving hand
Guiding me to choose.

If it were up to me
I would remain
Hidden.

Amongst the shadows
Of the wings of a vulture
That always seems to fly so close.

But when I think about being free
It's only you
I love the most.

So on today
I choose to walk away
From what was unfamiliar but comforting so.

I choose to live in strength.

D-Day,

Will be everyday.

Scripture

Ephesians 6:10 (NLT)

"A final word: Be strong in the Lord and in his mighty power."

Reflection

When was the day you decided to no longer live in the shadows and secrets of your abuser? When was the day you decided to allow God to be God and heal your soul? When was the day you felt your smile for the very first time? That day is your D-Day. Merriam-Webster defines D-Day as a military term for the day in which something important is planned or expected to happen. My first D-Day was the day I chose to surrender all of my worries, fears, and shame to God. My next D-Day was the day I said I would talk to a therapist about my sexual abuse history. My next D-Day was the day I chose to answer the call on my life. And I continue to have D-Day's everyday I wake up because I choose to stay in operation mode to be a free individual. All of the D-Day's that you will have throughout your lifetime will work towards the major operation, you being a soldier in the army of the Lord! Make your first D-Day today, will you?

Prayer

Lord, Your child is leaning on You to make her first D-Day today. For we know that as the decision is made to take a first step and activate Your healing, You will begin to put her life in motion towards living in freedom. God there is no one like You and I thank You for operating in the Spirit of abundance of knowledge, love, special forces, tactics, and weapons. You are the ultimate Commander-in-Chief and if we choose to follow and trust anyone to lead us to freedom, it is You! Let the special plan of operation You have already mapped out, manifest in Your daughter's life now, in Jesus' name.

Amen!

BUBBLE GUTS

For three days
I surrendered to the porcelain throne
Emptying my nerves and fears
Of what is to come.

Laughter and tears
Lows and highs
A clear mind and racing thoughts
A forced smile and a made-up glow.

All leading up to the ultimate
Plateau of a life
Which was considered an
Object.

Too many fears
Too many worries
So many prayers
So little time.

To move my feet
Step on a plane
Knock on a door
And open my mouth.

Open my mouth
To the man who ruined my life,
Ruined it
For the better.

I kneeled and let out a sigh
A Man picked me up when I spoke
"Talk to Me, I'm here to listen."
Tears rolled and words murmured.

I prayed the earnest prayer of my heart
"Lord, give me peace in my heart"
"Strength in my feet"
"And wisdom on my lips to speak."

Scripture

2 Corinthians 12:9-10 (NLT)

"Each time he said, "My grace is all you need. My power works best in weakness." So now I am glad to boast about my weaknesses, so that the power of Christ can work through me. That's why I take pleasure in my weakness, and in the insults, hardships, persecutions, and troubles that I suffer for Christ. For when I am weak, then I am strong."

Reflection

I was headed to confront my abuser. After 20 years I never thought I would take this journey. To a land full of brokenness, infested with hidden bombs, ready to explode at any moment. I didn't know that I would ever be ready and had it not been for God I don't believe I ever would have been. On the day of my flight to Los Angeles, I was nervous and full of empty emotions. My nerves were unending. I prayed the most earnest prayer I have ever prayed for strength, peace and wisdom. As I prayed, God lead me to read 2 Corinthians 12:9-10, and I smiled. In that moment, it was impressed upon my heart, I'm not doing any of this, God is! I don't have to think of the things to say to my abuser, God will! He calmed me as I continued to read the scripture over and over as an affirmation of what was to come. Whenever you need strength, all you need to do is lay your weaknesses on Him and His ability to wow you with His strength will calm your spirit. I am happy to be weak, because my God is strong!

Prayer

Lord, You are mighty and amazing in all that You do. Thank You for the strength You are giving my sister right now, to live her life in strength because in her weakness, she is strong through You. We honor You for being such a Father who is living. We ask You to cast out fear in our life as we travel along the path to freedom and healing. It's in Jesus' name we pray.

Amen!

STRENGTH ACTIVITY

To be a survivor of sexual abuse one is thought to be weak, fragile and unable to care for herself. She is thought to be unstable and evasive in life's hardest task. When in actuality, survivors of sexual abuse are one of the most resilient group of women on earth! To survive and press your way through life to bring you to a place of healing takes strength. I applaud you!

In Isaiah 41:10 (NLT) Isaiah wrote, "Don't be afraid, for I am with you. Don't be discouraged, for I am your God. I will strengthen you and help you. I will hold you up with my victorious right hand." You have your promise from your Father, God. He has given you the tools you need to strengthen your mind and your spirit to heal you from the strength-sapping grips of sexual abuse. You have resiliency whether you know it or not. We will engage those traits to positively catapult you into your next level of healing.

STRENGTH ACTIVITY

As survivors as sexual abuse, we know how to thrive and navigate through life, be resilient, but not necessarily to the function and degree that is positive and effective for our growth. For example, I am a very organized person, or so I like to think. Early on in my journey of healing, I would be sure to have everything under control, in its place, and operating at full function. If there was a fault, I would get nervous or upset and try to fix everything by myself. I was controlling because I could not control the sexual abuse that happened to me. It took time and practice for me to learn how to positively use the gift of organization in an effective way so it was not crippling my life. In today's activity, we will learn how to use our resiliency skills in positive ways.

1. **Maintaining healthy relationships** will allow those who love and care about you to support you. It's through healthy relationships that we are built up in hope and love, which increases our ability to be resilient.

2. **Recognize change is a part of life** and sometimes there is nothing you can do about it. Accepting change allows you to better adapt to your current circumstances and not be held victim to what could have been.

3. **Change your perspective** to what has happened to you. We cannot change the past but we can change our perspective on how we unravel and react to sexual abuse.

4. **Discover who you are today.** You are no longer a victim of sexual abuse. You are a woman who has survived a traumatic experiences and is healed in Jesus' name. Explore and ask the question, who am I today?

5. **Appreciate your life** because you are still living! I know there has been challenges in life that has kept you confused and bound but you are working through them now and you are still here!

6. **DO SOMETHING!** If you don't like how you feel as a result of sexual abuse, do something to change it. You have committed to taking the *Pathways to Healing* journey but healing does not stop here. Always be willing to problem solve situations in your life that you want to change.

7. **Keep your focus on the BIG picture** of life so when trivial situations occur you are not thrown off center.

8. **Take care of you** by doing activities you enjoy. Taking care of your mind and body will keep you in shape mentally and physically and prepared for when it is time for you to use your resiliency skills.

9. **Living as a survivor not a victim** will help you to keep an optimistic view of life. You also will have a greater value of yourself and become more appreciative to God throughout the remainder of your life!

TIME WITH GOD

Taking the time to reflect on the activity is necessary to fill your heart with peace and to build your muscles of strength. We will reflect today by praying and fasting with God (please read page ii for fasting guidance). Take time today to journal your thoughts and the instructions God will give you on how to build your strength in Him and in yourself.

In your personal time with God:

1. Read Philippians 4:13 to make your being a reality.
2. Begin to pray and ask God to reveal how He is your strength. Continue to seek Him about the ways you have been sapped of your strength in mind, body and spirit. Ask for solutions and strategies to release old ways that have impacted your ability to trust Him fully which gives you the strength you need to live this life.
3. Fast and meditate on your time spent with God today.

PURPOSE

AWAKE

i woke up today.

to the smiles and hugs of you.

i woke up today.

to the strength and the passion to do
all the things you have asked of me.

i woke up today.

from a slumber i have been in
since that dreadful day of hurt
which happened yesterday in my mind.

i woke up today.

to find joy in knowing
i have no reason to fear
the voices that tell me no
or the people who seem so big in stature.

i woke up today.

the scales came off my eyes
the chains came off my mind
and my mouth parted with

"I am ready."

Scripture

Romans 9:17 (NLT)

"For the Scriptures say that God told Pharaoh, 'I have appointed you for this very purpose of displaying my power in you and to spread my fame throughout the earth.'"

Reflection

God has appointed a time where you are awakened and just ready to move in sync with Him. It's like an amazing ballroom dance. He is the male leading you in the next step of the fox trot. In order for it to be a joyous, beautiful masterpiece, you have to follow His lead. If not, He will be dragging a rag doll and the masterpiece will be ruined. Open your heart and let Him guide you. He is the only One who knows how your dance will end. Give Him your hand, will you?

Prayer

Father, too often I am consumed with the what if's, with the next relationship, with the next bill or the next self-serving task. I release all hope, all power and every bit of my past, present and future to You. Help me to move my feet as You lead me. I trust You with all that I am. In Jesus' Name.

AMEN!

HIGH, HIGH, HIGH

Today I prayed
With everything in me
To reveal the true meaning of who I am.
I have nothing to offer
Other than my tattered heart.
So for what reason
Do You think I should stand apart?
In this homogenous universe
You chose me to do something new?
Every part of me wants to be in disbelief
But deep down I know it's true.
You gave me purpose
Before I was thought of.
Lord, You are the only One
Who knows what to do
With this tattered heart.
I trust that my purpose
Is wrapped up in You.
Help me to believe
That my future is true.
When You use every piece of me
I know my past will play a portion.
High is the bar
Of being an overcomer.

Not because I'm an over-achiever
But because You knew my mother
Would birth me into existence
As Your mouthpiece.

When I think of all of the parts
In the universe
You shifted for me
I choose to believe
I have a great destiny.

Thank You for understanding my feeble thoughts
I'm just so used to being a mangled heart.
Higher I will go
With You leading me.
I have purpose.

Scripture

Jeremiah 29:11 (NIV)

"For I know the plans I have for you," declares the Lord, "plans to prosper you and not to harm you, plans to give you a hope and a future."

Reflection

I have wondered my purpose for a long time. And what overshadowed me getting to a place where I was comfortable with my purpose was my sexual abuse. I felt like everywhere I went, every person I met, every career I thought about, every job interview I went on, every potential romantic partner, I would hear a voice screaming, "YOU NEED TO SAY SOMETHING ABOUT YOUR PAST!" It wasn't until I began to pray about this feeling to vomit my past on everyone that I met, God revealed to me I'm a mouthpiece of His goodness. I knew I would be an encouragement for women of sexual abuse but I thought that it would be as I met women from day to day in passing. As I would continue to pray about the ins and outs of my purpose, God began to show me visions and speak to me in my dreams. And one of them has manifested into this devotional. Don't let the fear of your past dictate your purpose being fulfilled. You don't know how many lives will be saved and added to the Kingdom by God uniquely using you. The call on your life is great, Satan tried to shut you up, BUT GOD! Keep praying for God to reveal His purpose for you, He will reveal it in His time. Everything you have experienced in your life will be used to the glory of God!

Prayer

Lord, You are so awesome in all of Your ways and Your ways are unique. I ask that You rain down Your purpose which is specific to Your daughter reading this. Give her peace and clarity about Your call on her life. Give her the resources and the means to be fully equipped to do Your work. Lord, I also ask You to give my sister patience as she waits to hear from You about her purpose. We know that fear and impatience will try to rise up against her therefore we cast it down in the name of Jesus. In Your time, she is ready to do Your work. I thank You for creating a beautiful soul, specifically for the work of Your Kingdom. I love You. In Jesus' name.

AMEN!

RAYS OF SON

He said, "You encourage me."
To be free.
He said, "I know I'm your dad."
"But you are teaching me a thing or two."
Tears began to fall.
I could only hear "who knew" in back of my mind.
God, I had no idea
Your love would shine through
A broken windowpane
Colored with various hues
Of black.
To represent every silent cry
Of my fearful encounters.
I never knew
The Son would shine through
Me
For others to see
Your healing power
Planted so deep.
My tears fall
And water more soil
Of another son or daughter
Who needs to be made whole.

Scripture

Matthew 5:16 (NLT)

"In the same way, let your light shine before others, that they may see your good deeds and glorify your Father in heaven."

Reflection

Believe it or not, God will place someone in your life to encourage and help during the healing process of sexual abuse. That someone happened to be my Dad. I told him how God placed it on my heart to write this devotional and just as a father would, he told me he was proud of me. I was happy enough with just that. But he continued on and said, "You know, you may not know this, but you encourage me, you really do." He began to ask questions about how my journey of healing has helped me in my life and ways he can find peace in his life. I was shocked! I never knew the power of walking in your purpose amongst your own. We always think about how we will impart wisdom upon others outside of the home, and never really think about our home. Our ability to affect the Kingdom with our purpose needs to first start in the home. God is amazing! Keep walking on the path He has paved out specifically for you. Sooner or later, someone will be curious of how you navigated your *Pathways To Healing*.

Prayer

Lord, we think so little of ourselves sometimes, we forget how powerful we can be when we are in line with Your Spirit. Lord, I am asking You to develop the vision and path You would have for Your daughter to walk along. For we know that our healing is not just for ourselves, it is for the Kingdom as well. I ask You to give Your daughter the discernment to know how to help walk others to freedom with her story. I thank You for all of the lives that will be changed and healed because of Your Holy Spirit. In Jesus' name.

Amen!

THE ARTIST

Ever thought about
How our bodies work?
How everything
Just, happens on its own?

Or so we think.
God is so intricate
He made us all to be
Full of His glory.

Heads turn
Eyes blink
Blood flows
To all the right places,
From head to toe.

Do you not believe
That you were created
Specifically,
To be a part of the Kingdom?

I know you see
A timid little girl
When you think about your misery.

Please know you are more than you see
You are a beautiful masterpiece
Just waiting to be
Breathed into
Like God did Adam & Eve.

God is so divine
He created you
To build His Kingdom
One life at a time.

Scripture

Psalm 147:4 (NIV)

"He determines the number of the stars and calls them each by name."

Reflection

Everything God has created is so cool when you think about it. Take for instance, our bodies. The human body is so complex yet so unique to each individual. In our bodies blood cells moves around to do numerous things, but most importantly to protect, cleanse and fight. When you get cut, blood cells rush to the injured site to build a wall and formulate blood clots to prevent you from bleeding out. Blood cells cleanse your body by taking waste to the kidney and liver which filter and clean the blood. Blood cells fight infections in your body by carrying antibodies to the site that is infected. Pretty cool huh? Blood cells have a very specific purpose to protect, cleanse and fight foreign objects in our system, 24 hours a day. Jesus did the same thing for each of us. By Him dying, His purpose is to protect us from ourselves and the enemy. Cleanse us from all pain and sin in our body and mind. And lastly, to fight the enemy when he attacks us. Pray to the Father for Him to reveal His specific purpose for you. Everything in this life has a purpose, including you!

Prayer

God, You are very intentional with Your love and Your creation. I'm asking You to open Your daughters' heart to Your unique purpose which was specifically created for her. Give her joy in knowing that she has life for a reason and her life is meaningful. I thank You in advance for the testimony of her life being fulfilled through You. Thank You for the power house of a woman she is. All glory belongs to You! In Jesus' name.

Amen!

AUTHOR DELICATE

Guilt, passion, freedom
All wrapped in one,
To take life seriously
Will mean there is no fun.

Sex, lies, smiles
All wrapped in three
Separate packages
That don't belong to me.

I feel such guilt
Every time I unwrap a package,
It's like the sender knows my soul.

I can tell someone hijacked these packages
And replaced them with negative contents,
I feel the attacks on my being,
As I continue to unpack it.

Guilt for the *sex* I enjoy having
With the *passion* I was given
To *free* my sister from the pain of her abuser
Who has been *lying*
To herself and others
With made-up *smiles*.

You see, I know those packages were intercepted
And rearranged with the labels of false conviction.
I was always meant to use its contents,
Just not for my personal gain.

Scripture

Psalm 139:23-24 (NIV)

"Search me, God, and know my heart; test me and know my anxious thoughts. See if there is any offensive way in me, and lead me in the way of everlasting."

Reflection

Every time after I had sex, I felt absolutely horrible. I was not married and I let God down, again. And in the moment, I knew I was better than what the encounter yielded, but I wanted to be wanted. As I began to grow in Christ, I realized the horrible feelings I would feel was not guilt, but it was conviction. Conviction and guilt, we often interchange the two. Conviction is used by God to heighten our senses to sin to bring us to repentance, whereas guilt recognizes the sin and then produces the feelings of fear, stagnation, and the impending doom of sin. God does not operate in guilt, He operates in conviction because He loves us and desires to see us whole in Him. Had I not continued to study, stay connected to ministry and repent when those convictions raised as a result of my actions, you would not be reading this devotional. It was through my convictions I realized I was set apart with purpose and was meant to witness to women who are survivors of sexual abuse who are possibly engaging in the same behaviors as I, physically, emotionally, relationally, mentally and spiritually. It was through my convictions I grew in passion for women who are hurting because of the abuse and hurting because of the behaviors they themselves have been repeating. Do not get your convictions confused with guilt. It is through your convictions the Holy Spirit can move to make an impact on you and the Kingdom. What are your convictions? Your convictions may very well be tied to your purpose. Strong convictions lead to change.

Prayer

Your love is marvelous. You are patient and loving to Your children. Thank You for clarity in the distinction of guilt and conviction, it is through this conviction we are able to clearly see You progressing our healing. I'm asking, in the name of Jesus for You to use those convictions to evoke change and purpose in Your daughter Lord. For this is where Your will and work will be done to push Your daughter to rise. In Jesus' name.

Amen!

PURPOSE ACTIVITY

Everyone on earth, including you, was birthed with a specific purpose in mind. Overtime, the self-defeatist mindset we have experienced as survivors is very much real. So real, we may have talked ourselves out of believing we have purpose. As you have read this week, you are always on God's mind and He desires to live through you, which is a part of His ultimate purpose for our lives.

Have you ever had someone tell you, "Oh my goodness, I think you will be great at (fill in the blank). Sometimes others see things in us which are natural, we rarely view great aspects of us as being a part of our purpose. This weeks activity will give us the opportunity to discover who we are in Christ.

PURPOSE ACTIVITY

In an effort to reveal you have purpose and to get things on track to tapping into your purpose, you will take a questionnaire on your spiritual gifts! The purpose of the questionnaire is to help you identify the spiritual gifts and talents God has placed in you. I have taken the same questionnaire and I've been pleasantly surprised with the results expressing exactly what my strengths are. Please set aside about 30 minutes to fully complete the questionnaire. Remember there is no right or wrong answer so be sure to select the first answer that resonates with you to give you accurate results.

www.gifts.churchgrowth.org

(On the right hand side of the site, please click, Spiritual Gifts Analysis)

TIME WITH GOD

Now that you have taken the spiritual gifts questionnaire, there is no better way to activate the results than personal prayer and fasting time with God (please read page ii for fasting guidance). Take time today to journal your thoughts on the results from your spiritual gifts questionnaire.

In your personal time with God,

1. Read Ephesians 3:12-14 to remind your why your are living this life, to serve Him.

2. Begin to pray and ask God to reveal His purpose for you and the discernment to know when He is speaking. Don't become frustrated if you don't hear an answer right away from God. Simply remain in prayer and be sensitive to your Guide, the Holy Spirit, in revealing the answer.

3. Fast and meditate on your time spent with God today.

FAITH

LOADS

You're everything to me.

Often times I forget
That You are my everything.
Only to remember
When I cry out to You

You're everything to me.

I'm forgetful and become consumed
With the what if's and is my life really true.
But as I close my eyes
And reflect on what brought me to my knees,
The one thing that reigns true is

You're everything to me.

Scripture

1 Peter 5:6-7 (NIV)

"Humble yourselves, therefore, under God's mighty hand, that He may lift you up in due time. Cast your anxiety on Him because He cares for you."

Reflection

God is everything. Everything. I know for me, sometimes when I get on my knees to pray, I have so much on my mind and I can only say, "You're everything to me." God can fix anything because He is everything. We conjure up and deal with so much from day to day, we forget no matter how big or small our problems, He can do it. God has not given you a worrying spirit, He gave you a calm and gentle spirit. As you spend time with Him today and you think about all you have to say or ask for, let Him know how much you need Him.

Prayer

No matter my load, heavy or light, Your desire is that I cast my load on You. Lord, help me to trust You with everything that I am. I'm afraid. I trust that Your perfect will will be done in my life as I trust You with every bit of my load. In Jesus' name.

Amen!

TRICKS

you show me happiness
you show me pain
you show me love
but all love is not the same
some love feels great
and makes you want to scream on the mountaintop
while other love is cold and bitter
yet with a loving hand.

you show me life
you show me death
you show me, me
ready to end it all
i cry and cower because I can't see me taking that fall
even though every fiber of me hates the way my life began
he spoke and said
"jump, its freeing."
frozen, I kept my eyes closed
praying away the urge to jump.

satan himself spoke to me to do the unthinkable
end this precious life
but there was one thing he forgot
on that mountaintop.
Jesus was tempted too
i told him, "you tried Jesus and He denied you."
little did he know
Jesus is my Savior and through Him
I WILL LIVE!

Scripture

Revelation 12:11 (KJV)

"And they overcame him by the blood of the Lamb and by the word of their testimony; and they loved not their lives unto the death."

Reflection

Satan likes to play games, tricks if you will, with the vulnerable. He speaks and he shows us images over and over again in attempts to get us to believe the things we see and hear are real. Ever listen to a song on the radio that you don't like, but you find yourself singing it because you hear it all the time? The enemy works the same way! He has no power and authority over you or anything that concerns you, it is us who gives him the power because we unknowingly begin to believe the tricks he whispers over and over again. Remember that God loves you and wants to see you healed. Any message that goes against that is a trick from Satan himself for you not to receive your healing. Pay attention to what you hear and see and trust the God that lives in you!

Prayer

Father, I come to You knowing Your Word is true and cannot fail. Right now, I plead the blood of Jesus over my mind, my life and anything that concerns me. Satan, you have no power and/or authority to influence who I am or the success of my healing and destiny. God, I relinquish all tricks, lies, and fears that the enemy has tried to get me to believe in my life unto You. I choose life, love and freedom in Christ. Thank You in advance for healing, strength and the discernment to recognize the voice of Satan. In Jesus' name.

Amen!

TWO LEAVES LIVING

Holes and bites
"Excuse my presentation,"
"I had no idea someone was joining me today."
As the day passes
Rays shine through, me.
Beautiful, bright, missing pieces of my being,
Showing my worth,
And the value You placed in me.
But the more I look to the left and right,
I see my neighbors beginning to look the same,
Tattered and hanging on.
I look ahead and I see
Me, in 10 years.
Bright, beautiful, and whole,
Yet connected to what seems like a thread.

"Care to join me?" She speaks.
I stretch to see who speaks.
"How are you keeping up with life?"
"Seemingly on the edge, but flourishing better than the rest of us?" I say.
"Although, it seems like I hang on to a thread
I have grown from there to here.
Holes, bitten, sometimes in pieces, and others trampling over me.
I got tired of being underneath.
Always second and expected to fall to my demise
But I had a story in my heart and accepted I was made to hang on.
Meant to hang on with every hole radiating the pure joy of my being.
I remember the day I took the first step, just like you
To be more than yesterday." She explains.

I heard a voice speak in the midst of my brave neighbor sharing her journey.
"You are connected.
Stepping to the edge is only proof
That you are ready to bloom.
To be the best you
I summoned you to be."

My new friend said,
"I took a chance, and here I am."
"So what's hard about being
In such a position of pressure and beauty?" Curiosity struck me.
"Remembering,
No matter what storm
May blow me from here to there,
I am still connected."

Scripture

Psalm 1:3 (NLT)

"They are like trees planted along the riverbank, bearing fruit each season. Their leaves never wither, and they prosper in all they do."

Reflection

I sat at the National Arboretum on a beautiful day. I sat under a tree with layers and layers of vines and branches with leaves bright and beautiful, full of chlorophyll. As I lay on my blanket with my hand behind my head, I began to notice, this beautiful tree had numerous leaves with holes and bite marks. As I continued to scan this lush tree, the closer the leaves were to the root of the branch and to the trunk of the tree, the more they were eaten, brown and tattered. I was baffled that such pattern was so uniform and seemingly odd. The closer the leaves were to the source the more nourished I thought these leaves would be. I began to scan for flourishing whole leaves, and to my surprise, they were on the edge. All of the full, beautiful, bright leaves were at the very end of each branch while connected to the vine. It was here God clearly said, sometimes in our lives we are beat up from being connected to God, people, family, our past, that we don't see the beauty in continued growth. By growing past where we think we are meant to stay in life, it's where we blossom and grow the most, at the very edge of comfort. Are you ready to grow and heal past this stage of comfort? Remember, you are still connected, even when you live on the edge.

Prayer

Lord, life is unpredictable at times and we often times don't know what is to come. Help us to trust You to surrender in faith and trust You to lead our lives from pain and distrust, to wholeness and trust. You are THE living God and the only One who can take our hand and lead us to the edge and protect us from falling. As we continue to grow and stretch our faith and trust in You, ease our fears. Thank You for the opportunity to grow with You by our side, every step of the way. Lead us Father, in Jesus' name.

Amen!

SAY WHAT?

"That will be $186.92."
But I don't have enough
What can I do to get these groceries?
I plot and scheme and wonder
How I was left with the short end of the stick.
After all I've been through?
My life.
My youth seized by uncle
Daddy left
Mom was busy working
Broke college student
And somewhere along the line
I gave my life to you.
I see so many
Full of evil and pleasantries of sin
But yet they prosper.

Say what?

I have no understanding
Of my meekness
Being devoured
By those who prey on the gentle dove
I am for you?

Say what?

Healing
Celibacy
A steward over a little
To be trusted with much
I can't believe You give others trust
Yet they curse You
Or maybe not devout
I thought Your children were to prosper
What's this about?

Scripture

Psalm 73:16-18 (NLT)

"So I tried to understand why the wicked prosper. But what a difficult task it is! Then I went into your sanctuary, O God, and I finally understood the destiny of the wicked. Truly, you put them on a slippery path and send them sliding over the cliff to destruction. Truly, you put them on a slippery path and send them sliding over the cliff to destruction."

Reflection

The wickedest Christian or perhaps non-Christian seem to prosper right? They have everything we as Christian survivors are suffering for everyday. We suffer for financial freedom, a wonderful home, beautiful families, a great career, a loving husband that we waited all of our life for, and the list can go on. There are so many instances that can disqualify someone from receiving the blessings to be poured on them daily, including your abuser. But as a believing survivor, your worry is not the riches and prosperity of someone else, your worry is your walk with God. Works and wealth do not define who you are. It shines the light on WHOSE you are. Everything you have, material and intangible, is because of Christ and no doing of your own. Acknowledge the blessing on your life, healing and peace, instead of your rightful portion. Besides, your treasure is not here on earth, it lays in heaven (Matthew 6:19-21 NIV).

Prayer

God, Your daughter has been through so much and is depending on You to bring her to the other side of victory in things that she has been believing You for. Our prayer is that You give her the focus and determination of an eagle when it comes to living for Your Kingdom. The life of the wicked has already been determined by You, so we worry not. Shift our focus to living for You and You getting glory in everything we do. In Jesus' name.

Amen!

HE FIGHTS

I'm hurting
Don't you see,
I have been beaten
By the hands of someone
Who could care less for me.
Truth be told
I'm rather numb
From his harsh hands
And aggressive pulls.
But more so from you watching me
Withstand the years of manipulation,
Confusion of love and lust at its finest.
Weeping for no apparent reason
While flashes of secret hiding places haunt me.
You are the reason I stand tall
In my mind
But I can't help think
Why didn't You stop this?
I deserve an answer
To the bystander You were
Protection and peace were not upon me.

                    Who said I was an innocent bystander?
               My heart hurt every time you received a strike.
                  Or was caressed behind closed doors.
                        My Spirit lives in you,
                            And cried every tear.
                      Felt every pierce in your heart.
                      Every nightmare you dreamed.
                    I fought for the path before you
           To be clear of visions of loneliness and tears.
                Because my Holy Spirit lives in you
                    My fight has already been won.
              The days you felt peaceful comfort,
       My Holy Spirit fought the enemy and won.

Scripture

Deuteronomy 20:4 (NLT)

"For the Lord your God is going with you! He will fight for you against your enemies, and he will give you victory!"

Reflection

I wondered why God 'allowed' me to be sexually abused. I wondered for a very long time if He saw everything that happened. Silly thing to say right? Well, if God is omnipresent and can do anything why didn't He rescue me? A question I asked myself was, 'who says He didn't see everything that happened?' 'Who says He hasn't rescued me?' I began to think and have a dialogue with God and He said, "I'll fight for you." In times when we thought God was not there, He was. In times where we wished someone would notice what was going on, He was there. God hurts when we hurt because a piece of Him lives in us, Holy Spirit. Holy Spirit was sent to you to be a "big brother" to protect and guide you until Christ's return. And because He lives in you, He has won the fight! It may not seem like justice has been served because everything happened to you, but God kept you by sending the Holy Spirit. It's up to us to acknowledge His presence and let Him continue to fight on our behalf.

Prayer

Lord, it's been a tough road. A tough road that has lead to questions of if You were there or not. But God! We acknowledge You see and know everything and was down on Your knees with us everytime we cried out to You. Thank You for sending Holy Spirit to comfort and keep us in times of despair. For we know because Holy Spirit lives in us, we are free to trust that You are our protection. Thank You, we ask these things in Your Son's name.

Amen!

FAITH ACTIVITY

Ephesians 2:8 and Romans 12:3 explain we were all given a measure of faith. If you didn't recognize you had faith, know that it has been in you since the day you were born again. It is through your faith God can work effectively in and through your life.

Thinking about life, sometimes we put so much emphasis on the outcome and overlook the strategy. With an end result ahead of you and no strategy to get there can be very dangerous. Your faith is the exact tool that you need to have a fail-proof strategy to get you through anything in life which will maintain your level of hope in our Father.

FAITH ACTIVITY

To keep your measure of faith in pristine shape, there are a few things you can do. In making sure your faith is in tip-top shape, the number one goal is to be consistent. Joshua 1:8 says, "Study this Book of Instruction continually. Meditate on it day and night so you will be sure to obey everything written in it. Only then will you prosper and succeed in all you do." Therefore, we have to connect daily with God. In today's exercise, here are a few tips on how to connect with God daily:

1. Devote a time, everyday, where you spend time with God. The time of day can be anytime that you are able to get somewhere quiet and hear from God.

2. Read your Word based on a topical devotional, such as *Pathways to Healing*, by reading chapters, or simply reading from the beginning to the end of the Bible. Once you complete your reading for that day, pray and ask God to speak.

3. Spend some quiet time, literally, and wait to hear God to give you clarity on what you read and prayed about. Ask for instructions specifically on what He needs you to do for the day.

It is in our quiet time that we gain insight and perspective on the things that concern God. He is able to talk to us and clearly delineate His plan. Don't take this time for granted. As you do this consistently, over time your faith will increase and cause you to grow in wisdom and faith in Christ.

TIME WITH GOD

Being consistent and devoting time to God in our busy and distracting lives can be difficult. But it is only through this time that we can hear our Father and gain invaluable tools for our day. Today, we will take the time to specifically ask God to exercise our faith through reading the Word, praying and fasting on the word He will give you (please read page ii for fasting guidance).

1. Read Psalm 119:18.

2. Pray and ask God to open your eyes to the Word as you read it daily. Ask Him to reveal the areas in your life that may be blocking Him from speaking clearly to you to increase your faith. When God gives you those areas, be sure to write them down and pray and ask God how to release those things from your life.

3. Fast and meditate on your time spent with God today.

TRUST & FORGIVENESS

I DON'T WANT TO

After all is said and done
I am left here to deal
with
you
Plaguing my mind
Infesting my behavior
Terrorizing my emotions
Aborting my dreams
Truly, I have no more space
To even consider
How to overcome all of the memories
You forced into my brain
Your infamous scenes
Of my rated X childhood reality TV series
Play day in and day out
In my synaptic movie player
That once was called a brain

I don't want to give you freedom
While I am held captive to myself
What kind of justice system is this

I don't want to give you restful nights
And peaceful dreams

I don't want to give you a piece of me
That is at risk again
Of being used and rejected

I don't want to give you

Forgiveness.

Scripture

Matthew 18:21-22 (NLT)

"Then Peter came to Him and asked, "Lord, how often should I forgive someone who sins against me? Seven times?" "No" Jesus replied, "seventy times seven."

Reflection

With that scripture, I know you are saying "God is funny!" I know how you feel, because I said it too. As a survivor, you don't want to forgive anything your abuser has done. You didn't ask to be violated, nor did you ask for the horrible pain and memories you have been left with. What gives someone of horrible existence the right to be forgiven? In all actuality, according to man, they have NO right to be forgiven for what they have done to you. But as a believer who is seeking healing, where do you think the healing begins? It begins with you, forgiving and handing it over to God. I remember the day I knew God was calling me to forgive my abuser. It weighed on me so heavy because I felt as though I was caving in yet again to his pseudo power that has been strong over me for years. If I forgive, I'm weak and everyone will know it. But I was given this word by God, "I have so much for you to live for and you are not living." It hit me. The more I harbored anger and the memories of the unforgiveable acts of sexual abuse, the more I realized I was allowing my abuser to live a legacy in me for free. I felt free days after I decided to forgive because there was so much I said I would never do because of the abuse. I vowed I would never have children because I was afraid of my baby girl or my precious son being abused. Had I not turned it over to God, I would not have been free from his control and I would not be able to say today that I can't wait to have children! Because Christ commands us to forgive, I know you want to know, "what is in it for me?" What's in it for you is peace, clarity and the freedom to live beyond your wildest dreams!

Prayer

God, my sister is hurting. I understand her pain of wanting to hold her abuser captive, and what has been done to her for so long. I pray that You begin to work a change in her heart and in her mind, to have her live in freedom as You have designed her to live. Touch her in the places that are in deep pain and deep fear of what is to come upon forgiveness. Give her peace beyond her understanding that will transcend beyond her human capacity to understand. I trust Your will of forgiving and being free is already done. In Jesus' name.

AMEN!

HER

Late mornings and early nights
It seemed to be her thing.
Anthony Hamilton's-Float plays
As she is ready to be anything he likes.
She loves how she makes him feel
Like a woman who just watched someone else win a marathon.
High from the miles of smiles and hugs
That has taken her around the world in her mind.
She loves how she keeps a flow of supply
For seemingly endless use.
To never turn away
Her most tolerant bidder.
But she began to feel empty
It seems as though she is running low.
But never to the hands of a crook
Who took advantage of her pre-mature experience
In love and respect-onomics.
I heard she committed herself
And constantly thinks of her secret acts.
Who is she to believe she will ever be set free
From all of the late mornings and early nights?

I have to be honest
Her is me.
And I love sex.
Sex with the wrong one
Sex with the right one
As long as he is true to me.
The only girl he cares about
In that moment.
Truth is
I hate me.
Because really
I don't know how to love with my heart
Only with my sacred treasure.
"Love" hurt me
And I'm only replaying what I see.
Shameful acts
And appalled deeds
I just want to get the point
Where I forgive her,
Who is really me.

Scripture

Philippians 3:13 (NLT)

"No dear brothers and sisters, I am still not all I should be, but I am focusing all of my energies on this one thing: Forgetting the past and looking forward to what lies ahead."

Reflection

I remember the day I realized I had a problem with sex. My ex-boyfriend said to me, "don't give it up the first time someone asks for it." Well THAT slapped me in the face, and he only ATTEMPTED to have sex with me. He got up and walked through the door after he spoke those real words to me before he left. I felt the pie sliding down my face as I sat there and watched my door slam and him walk through it. How could I not see I had a problem that was being fed by all of the negative love that I received as a child? Of course I wouldn't see it! I didn't know that I was giving my love freely, I thought that it's what two people in love do. Am I the only one who had that moment when I realized that I had done something that was out of my "normal" character due to a heightened sense of sexuality? Thank you for not leaving me hanging sister! Be understanding and forgiving to yourself that you were exposed and unknowingly trained to act in the manner in which you acted sexually. You may even feel guilty for the sexual arousal that you experienced during sexual acts that you did not permit. Understand, our bodies were made to react to sexual stimulus and just because your body responded, against your minds will, does not mean the sexual abuse that took place was right. Forgiving yourself for all of the negative behaviors because of the abuse is a must. Why you ask? It's the only way you will heal for yourself and know when to engage and enjoy pure sexual encounters in the future!

Prayer

Lord, I know that I have willingly done wrong because of the sexual experiences that I was exposed to. I am asking You right now to forgive me for all that I have done to defile my body, which is Your temple. Lord, I pray that You heal my heart and shield it from further pain. Heal my mind and remove all images and acts I have committed from memory that may be taunting me. Please allow me to feel Your love and forgiveness as I forgive myself and others. In Jesus' name.

AMEN!

LOCKED UP

I sit here in my cell
I can't believe I did the unthinkable.
Who am I
That I might sin against Your own children?

I stand with my hands
On the cold bars
Shaking them back and forth,
As though I don't hold the key
To set myself free.

I stand in silence
Remembering all that was done to me,
A pretty, innocent girl.
I stand in silence
Remembering all I have done
To bring back that
Pretty, innocent girl.
Party, Smoke, Sex, Porn,
All sit in the jail cell with me.

As I turn to take a seat
Unforgiveness hovers over me,
I tried to sit
But so uncomfortable I was,
I realized this was more than I could bear.

I reached into my pocket
And took a look at the key
That unlocks the door
To set me free.
"I don't belong here"
I heard myself say
I keep toiling
But today will be the last day.

I took the key and turned the lock,
As I stepped out to freedom
I heard Unforgiveness say,
"Forget me not!"
I was scared
Because we shared the same cell for so long.
How could I leave a friend and not feel remorse?
I kept walking towards freedom,
I realized, I've always had a choice.

Scripture

John 8:36 (ESV)

"So if the Son sets you free, you will be free indeed."

Reflection

We have been in jail to ourselves for so long. We have been held hostage by the abuse of our past that we have become so unaware we hold the keys to our freedom. On the particular day I was writing this devotional, I was praying for healing for women who have been sexually abused. I was also praying for forgiveness for some of the things I have done in my life as a result of the abuse. Although the abuse drove the behaviors, I still needed to take responsibility for what I did. God showed me as a prisoner holding on to the bars of my cell looking out. But there were 'people' in my cell with me and the biggest person was unforgiveness. Not just for my abuser but for me too. To forgive myself for what I have done in my life that has violated who I am and what my Father stands for. What are you holding on to that you need to forgive yourself for? I charge you to set yourself free from the lies of the enemy telling you, you will never make it through the pain or God will never forgive you.

Prayer

God, Your daughters' heart is reeking with unforgiveness. We know that forgiveness is a process but I am asking You, right now in the name of Jesus, to expedite the process. You are a God of no time and I'm asking that You move on my sisters' behalf quickly to bring her to a place of freedom and a place of peace. Set her free Lord! I trust and believe her jail cell has been demolished and she is walking in freedom now! In Jesus' Name.

Amen!

I HAVE IT ALL

I'm dying on the inside
I don't know what to do
Weight room strength
And the prayers of others
Won't fix me moving my own feet.

Challenges day after day
Careless abusive family member
Have tainted the view of myself.

Studying and reading books
To gain a knowledge and understanding
Of who I am to the Most High
It's like, in one ear and out the other
I choose to live blind.

Until I saw the truth
Written clearly in thin air
I have been equipped with arsenal
Through years of studying
The only thing is
I was too afraid to move my feet.

Little woman
Left, right, left,
Look back over your life
And realize
God has not left you alone
He lives within you.

Open your eyes and see
It's trust in yourself
That's keeping you
From walking freely
Right into destiny.

Scripture

Ephesians 6:10-13 (NLT)

"A final word: Be strong in the Lord and mighty in his power. Put on all of God's armor so that you will be able to stand firm against all strategies of the devil. For we are not fighting against flesh-and-blood enemies, but against evil rulers and authorities of the unseen world, against mighty powers in the dark world and against evil spirits in heavenly places. Therefore, put on every piece of God's armor so you will be able to resist the enemy in time of evil. Then after the battle you will be standing firm."

Reflection

How many times do you reach out to others to tell you what you already know? Or better yet, you simply forget that you have the knowledge and equipment to command your life? Often times, our trust in ourselves is shot as survivors of sexual abuse. Our ability to believe the God in us to take us to the other side of sorrow is non-existent at times. How much longer will you allow the painful memories of your past to determine your ability to live in freedom? God has equipped you to live in His beautiful land in peace and abundance. Trust there is power living in you through the Word of God and you are the only one who can activate it daily to accomplish and navigate your *Pathways to Healing*.

Prayer

Lord, thank You for removing the blinders off of us as we walk through life not trusting ourselves with the knowledge and power You have given us. Remind us often, all of the lessons You have taught us so we may utilize it to command our lives and fight against the enemy as he attempts to rise against us. Thank You for a new direction in You. In Jesus' name.

AMEN!

SONG & DANCE

I take one step
He takes two
Do-si-do now
Take his cue.

Slap your knees
Twirl and twirl
Show your colors
You beautiful girl.

I take one step
He takes two
Do-si-do now
Take his cue.

Tap your feet
Smile real big
Someone loves you
You sexy kid.

I take one step
He takes two
Do-si-do now
Take his cue.

Spin and jump
And play all day
That's how abusers
Have their way.

Scripture

2 Timothy 3:13 (NLT)

"But evil people and imposters will flourish. They will deceive others and will themselves be deceived."

Reflection

Not all abusers are big, mean, and ugly. Some are fun, happy, handsome/pretty and just not the person who fits the description of "someone who would do that." Some of us fell into the arms of a very loving fun person who mistreated us, as a child or as an adult. If this was the way your abuse occurred, through play, know that it is still not your fault. Manipulation and trust was used to take advantage of you. Your ability to trust other people who fit the description of a happy and fun loving person may alarm you. I rebuke the effects of your abuse from seeping into your ability to make friends and trust others.

Prayer

Lord, my sister was taken advantage of, in ways that are indescribable. But most importantly, her soul was taken. I am asking that You take her soul and ignite it anew. Remove all negative behaviors, manipulation, and mistrust that was used to take advantage of her which she has now taken on. Give her strength, peace and joy as she seeks to replace joyous yet abusive memories of her childhood. Keep her in perfect peace. Restore her trust in people Lord. In Jesus' name.

Amen!

TRUST & FORGIVENESS ACTIVITY

This is not a place of embarrassment, shame, guilt, defeat or emptiness. This is a place of restoration, peace, strength, confidence, joy and overcoming the depths of your past! As we embark on opening up to forgiving our abusers and trusting ourselves, please keep an open mind and know that this will happen in your time. There is no pressure to forgive your abuser today.

According to Colossians 3:13 (NLT), "Try to understand other people. Forgive each other. If you have something against someone, forgive him. That is the way the Lord forgave you." In this same vein, we are not exempt from forgiving our abusers. Some survivors feel as though, if they forgive their abuser they are condoning the abuse or the abuser is not being held accountable for his/her actions. This could not be farther form the truth.

I know you have heard the phrase, "forgiveness is not for the other person, its for you." Not forgiving someone causes us not to receive what God has for us because our hands are not in a position to receive. Imagine you are excited about giving a gift to your mother and she stands before you excited. You hand her a bright and shiny new 24k gold 6ct tennis bracelet that she has always wanted but she is holding on to an old, cracked cubic zirconia bracelet she believes is the real thing. Not that there is anything wrong with cubic zirconia, but it simply is not the real thing. Your mother would be holding on to false truths.

As we are able to forgive the things of our past, we are able to learn how to trust ourselves and others. Over the years, you probably have recognized that it has not been easy to trust family, friends, romantic partners, colleagues and/or yourself. John 14:1 (NLT) specifically calls us to, "Don't let your hearts be troubled. Trust in God, and trust also in me." Trusting seems like a heart aching and fearful choice, sort of like forgiveness.

Having walked this same pathway, I remember "trusting" people, only to discover that I never trusted people, I was defensive. I allowed other people to open up to me but I never allowed myself to be vulnerable and open up to them. We are called to be in relationship with each other (Romans 12:5), but in order to be in relationship, we have to learn how to trust.

Offering trust and forgiveness does not warrant that the person will change but it will change the blessings you will receive. Walk towards freedom with me and make an imperative choice for your health, mind, body and spirit.

TRUST & FORGIVENESS ACTIVITY

Perhaps you need to forgive a family member who condoned the abuse, knowingly and unknowingly, your abuser, or most importantly yourself. Too often as a result of the abuse, we engage in undesirable behaviors or gain discreditable characteristics that we are deathly ashamed to admit. As we continue with today's exercise, keep your heart grounded but release the shame, fear, pain and regret.

For this exercise you will need the following:

- Notebook paper cut into cubes
- Pen
- Bowl
- Water

INSTRUCTIONS

1. Fill your bowl with water.
2. Write on each piece of paper, as many as you want, things, people or situations that are holding you back from forgiving your abuser, yourself, or someone who knowingly or unknowingly condoned the abuse. Be honest (i.e. shame, fear, pleasure, sex, mother, father, money, secrets, etc.).
3. Once you have written everything down, fold each piece of paper and submerge them in the bowl of water and watch them become covered.
4. Now take the bowl and pour your water into the toilet.
5. Finally, flush!

As you watched each piece of paper become submerged and covered with water, remember that these things no longer have substance. You can try to reach back in and take out each piece of paper, but it no longer has value and form, just like the abuse of your past. Be mindful as you are on your *Pathways To Healing*, you may want to pick back up the things you have flushed away today. Each time you want to pick back up these things, let today serve as a gentle reminder, they are flushed away from your future and are gone forever.

TIME WITH GOD

In your time with God today, seek His wisdom in regards to trust and forgiveness. Recognize that forgiveness is releasing a debt. We can attempt to intellectualize or make excuses for the abuse, however, taking either action will simply mask us getting to the root of our hurt. Through years of manipulation, hearing your truth meter clearly takes some time. Today we will go before our Father and ask for a recalibration of our ability to trust and forgive the right people, and the ability to trust ourselves, through prayer and fasting (please read page ii for fasting guidance). Lean in on God and His wisdom if this is rough for you. Take the following steps as you bring trust and forgiveness before God:

1. Read Proverbs 10:12 and John 16:12-15.

2. Be specific in your prayers and ask God how He wants you to move towards freedom through forgiveness. Pray and ask God if it is safe for you to offer forgiveness to your abuser through various means of communication (i.e. in person, letter, e-mail, text, Skype etc.). Your journey will look different from everyone else. Speak to Him and let Him know the reason why you desire to keep your feelings and ability to trust, to yourself.

3. Fast and meditate on your time spent with God today.

RESTORATION

FREEDOM

I choose peace.
I choose love.
I choose honor.
I choose grace.
I choose freedom.

freedom to be
the woman you created me to be
without the shadows of
doubt
fear
and thoughts of those moments
that my freedom to be a happy girl
was taken from me.

I choose forgiveness.
I choose to surrender.
I choose humility.
I choose freedom.

only you can free this mind.
only you can free this caged spirit.
my joy rests in you.

and as you ask me
to lay my burdens down
i freely say "i do".

Scripture

Galatians 5:1 (NIV)

"It is for freedom that Christ has set us free. Stand firm, then, and do not let yourselves be burdened again by a yoke of slavery."

Reflection

Honey there is nothing better than being FREE! Being free to be the unique person God molded you to be. Free from the traps of what your past yielded you. Free from the grips of your sanity slipping between your delicate hands. Free from the lies people have engrained in your mind. Free from the lies you have engrained in your mind. FREE! Your path of being restored is upon you. But it takes you embracing the pain, embracing the fear, embracing the possibility of meeting a new woman after your journey of healing. Who is this new woman you ask? You!

Prayer

Father, I pray that Your daughter keeps focus on You as she walks in freedom. Lord, You have promised us freedom yet it is up to us to stand firm, believing You have already set us free from the traps and fears of our past. Thank You for a solid foundation that has been built for my sister to stand upon without the fear of wavering to and fro. Hallelujah to Your name and praises to You for showing my sister her path of restoration and freedom! In Jesus' name.

AMEN!

RESTORE ME

i've been broken
to pieces that are unrecognizable.
the young woman

who found joyin the wind
blowing on a sunny day
is buried under the rubble
of violence, fear, tears, and pain

i have fought for so long
i even fight in my sleep

restore my peace daddy
restore my dreams
restore my joy
restore me to the time
when i didn't know
what it felt like to be used

i feel my mind setting free

as i pray to you
you gently remind me

i am restoring you now
the first steps of restoration
started when you asked me
restore my peace daddy
i came running.

Scripture

Isaiah 42:16(ESV)

"And I will lead the blindin a way that they do not know,in paths that they have not knownI will guide them.I will turn the darkness before them into light, the rough places into level ground.These are the things I do,and I do not forsake them."

Reflection

Remember when you had no fear of being around people? It gave you such joy to run free as a young lady. What happened to her? She still lives but it takes the gut-wrenching act of praying to God for healing and then taking the first step. In all your pain, confusion, and fear, on the other side of that step is restoration. Find the strength to know when it's not you or God speaking. Trust the God in you!

Prayer

Lord, your daughter wants to be made new again. She is wanting to break free from the misery of her past sexual abuse. With You Father, all things are made new and we ask for a special blessing of restoration upon Your daughter, where she feels joy, peace, security, once, and love. To move her confidently into her purpose filled future. Thank You for restoration. In Jesus' name.

Amen!

CHIPS & SCRAPS

Yellow, black, red
All to the tune of mute.
Orange, yellow green
To the sound of nothing.
Remnants of me
Bright and vibrant
Trying to come together
To make a peaceful pattern
That flows on the dance floor
As I twirl.

No thread pieces together
So many frays and odd pieces
Sides are measured
And rocks begin to fall from the fabric
Pulverized to dust and a pile stands
At the foot of my Seamstress.

"These colors and patters don't match
So I'll bring a few more next week."
He smiled as He began to speak.
"I can use what we have
I've never seen such beauty."

Sides are measured
Hand and foot begin to work
And patterns begin to form.
I only wish I had a few things to add
Like fine linen and silk
Soft to the touch
All of my chips and scraps
Look like it won't be enough.

My Seamstress stops,
It's like my thoughts were spoken aloud,
"Leave the creativity up to Me
All of the chips and scraps are enough."

Hands and feet move faster
And a masterpiece is being made
Right before my eyes
To twirl and dance with such grace
On the dance floor of life
He places the pieces of me of my hand
And speaks,
"Put this on, and remember My name
And refer others to Me
Tell them to bring Me their pieces too
It brightens My heart to see
You proudly wear pieces of you
Stitched together by Me."

Scripture

Hosea 6:1 (NLT)

"Come let us return to the Lord. He has turned us to pieces; now he will heal us. He has injured us; now he will bandage our wounds."

Reflection

How many pieces of chips and scraps do you have laying around? Laying around in so many different places that you may have even forgot where they are. On my journey of healing, I have come to know that God uses everything we have been through. Everything is used as a lesson or as a tool for Him to get the glory in your life. But most importantly, for you to live in freedom. Bring ALL of you to God. Every single piece of you, even pieces that don't make sense, and watch Him weave together pieces, by the threads of Him, for you to walk boldly and gracefully onto the dance floor of life.

Prayer

God, our tattered hearts, beat up feet, weary minds and empty souls need You. You are the only One who can use everything we have and turn it into a designer piece. Right now, we worship and thank You for everything You are doing and have done to restore our seemingly useless pieces. I ask that You reveal every piece of my sister that needs Your special thread to sow her back together in torn places. Thank You for the wonderful garment that she will wear with pride. Thank You that others will see You as she wears her special garment with confidence. We honor You as the Master Seamstress, who uses every piece of our lives to bring us to freedom. In Jesus' name.

Amen!

TEMPLE BUILDER

I keep my distance sometimes
Afraid of what I might look like
If I let You completely rearrange me.

Taking me to the next level
Beyond my comprehension
Shining amongst celestials and queens.

You building my temple
To Your perfect measurements
Without my participation
As You *cut, stretch, mold, nail and glue.*

My insides tremble,
"What are You doing?!"
"OUCH!!!"
"I don't like that!"
"Why would You do it like that?"

I have no response from You
Initially.
You keep working
Spin me around
And whisper in my ear.

"Your *cut* was to free you
From the memories of your awful past
And give you the *strength*
You need to move your feet
So I can *mold* your mind daily
To see why I *nailed* my Son to the cross
To *glue* your life back together."

Scripture

Romans 8:37 (NLT)

"No, despite all things, overwhelming victory is ours through Christ, who loved us."

Reflection

It's crazy how we honestly believe some of the things we go through in life is not for our benefit. Grant it, it's not fun when things happen, but take a step back. Has anything ever happened to you that has not turned around for your benefit? Maybe you need to review your life from God's lenses. Take hope sis. Everything God is doing in your life is a step closer to you moving towards victory in your life!!!

Prayer

God, we declare victory over our lives right now. Although we don't understand why we have gone through the pains of our past, we ask that You ease our fears and pain of You rebuilding our lives in our favor. Teach us how to trust You because no Father will forsake or harm their child. You are marvelous in all that You do and we cast out all fear to grow into the beautiful woman You intend for us to be. All the glory belongs to You for turning a broken spirit into a splendid woman. Thank You in advance for restoration and peace! It's in Your Son's name we pray.

Amen!

GARAGE SALE

YO!
What is going on?!
This is my stuff!
What gives YOU the right to sell it!?

I want to cry as I see everything from my life
Laid strategically on linen
To make my past look pretty.

"Everything is for sale!" she yells.

Who's this lady?
It's like my life has been packed
In a compact format
For everyone to easily come
And pick what they like.

I'm too embarrassed
As I walk down the table
To see all of what she got.
OH NO!
Please don't tell me…..
She did get everything!

My heart races and I want to hide
Pornography
Lies
Secrets
Little god's
All lined up, neatly
Like tchotchkes.

I woke up from this horrible dream
Appreciating its worth
Everything must go
Under His submission.

My life is not my own
And liberty I seek
Let everyone take what they want
Those things never belonged to me.

Scripture

Psalm 90:8 (NLT)

"You spread out our sins before you—our secret sins—and you see them all."

Reflection

I woke up filled with anxiety wondering who this mysterious lady was who knew ALL of my secrets and so was casual in laying everything out there. I then grasped, as I have submitted my life to Christ and asked Him to make me whole, there were things I needed to get rid of. As your journey to a peaceful place of healing begins to speed up, what needs to go on the auction block? What treasured sins do you need to get rid of? Allow God to search your heart through and through to expose everything that is not like Him. It is only through the light shining in darkness are we able to be made whole again.

Prayer

Father, we come before You asking for forgiveness. Forgiveness for the things we have done that is not pleasing in your sight and has kept us from being ever so close to You. God we thank you for being gracious enough to allow us back into Your presence and be washed clean in Your blood. We take it not lightly the opportunity to be made whole in Your Kingdom. Lord, we bind the hand of the enemy who is trying to keep us gripped to any generational curses or proclivities that would keep us in bondage and separated from Your love and restoration. We thank You and we love You for all You are doing and have done in our lives. Please show us how to accept Your grace and Your love. It's in Jesus' name we pray.

Amen!

RESTORATION

To be built up, torn down and repaired to original construction is the epitome of restoration. Notice the definition includes, "repaired to original construction", which means the foundation and structure was built with a purpose.

You were not created to be defeated and torn down, you were created to thrive. Sexual abuse was intended to kill you but God's grace has kept you. Repairs include, ripping up, nailing, throwing away and for some time, being in an 'unfinished' state.

The greatest part of restoration is the end result. It may not look like you are able to continue on this *Pathways to Healing*, but the amazing part has just begun, your rebuilding.

RESTORATION ACTIVITY

In today's activity, the focus of our restoration process will be surrendering. It is at the point of surrender, that we can fully be restored back to who God intended us to be. In Psalm 37:7 (GW), "Surrender yourself to the LORD, and wait patiently for him. Do not be preoccupied with [an evildoer] who succeeds in his way when he carries out his schemes." Notice the scripture says, "wait patiently for him". Surrendering EVERYTHING to God after all you have experienced through abuse will take time. But God's promise in Joel 2:25 gives us hope.

For this exercise you will need the following:

1. Glass
2. Water
3. Spoon
4. Ingredients in your spice cabinet (6-7 spices will do)

INSTRUCTIONS

1. Take your glass and fill it half-way with water.
2. Begin to put a dash of everything from your spice cabinet you have selected into the glass of water.
3. Take your spoon and stir the ingredients until completely mixed together.
4. Now drink! (Just kidding)
5. Take your glass and put it under the kitchen water faucet.
6. Turn your faucet on and begin to allow the fresh to water push out all of the ingredients in the glass until the water runs clean.

Just like the glass of ingredients, so often we allow the symptoms and pain of our past to be mixed together and we deliberately drink it everyday. It's like we are serving ourselves a does of pain daily when we choose not to surrender everything in our past over to Christ. It's only through surrendering can we be washed clean and made whole, resorted back to our original function, which was symbolized by the water running clean. Through surrendering, it takes time to be restored to clear everything out of us that does not belong. Remember, Holy Spirit was always dwelling in you (the glass of water), it just took time for Him to become clear to you.

TIME WITH GOD

Restoration can take much more time and money because in order not to damage the original structure that is standing, you have to be diligent and careful. But removing what no longer is useful and to replace it with items that are more suitable, is so rewarding when the finished product is complete. Through prayer and fasting today (please read page ii for fasting guidance), God will reveal to you His desires to do a work in you, which will remove all negative thoughts and feelings:

1. Read Luke 8:38-48.

2. Pray to God about your desire to be resorted, just like the woman with the issue of blood. It was her trust and faith in God that made her whole, even though she was considered a pest to the community. Ask Him to reveal to you areas in your life that need restoration and to give you the ability to accept the wisdom to work through your restoration.

3. Fast and meditate on your time spent with God today.

BEAUTY

SEASHELLS

You were left behind
To rot, and live no more.
You were left behind
To fend for the very things
That give you life
Your beauty and uniqueness.
You were left behind
To be used for what one
Or YOU thought would be of no use.

You were left behi....

.... NO! you were never left behind
I repurposed you for what you thought as,
'What can He do?'

You were.....

But as far as the naked eye could see
No one understood you but Me,
You were not left behind
I chose you, specifically.

To be free!
To be used for My glory!
To be changed for my victory!
No one knew that
You were washed ashore
To be picked up by ME.

Scripture

Romans 8:11 (NLT)

"Therefore, there is now no condemnation for those who are in Christ Jesus."

Reflection

As I sat and reflected on the seashore one morning, something was revealed to me by looking at seashells. Seashells are empty caucuses of animals washed up on the shore. Most people use them to throw at others or they are simply overlooked and stepped on. To be a pointless ornament, that our sexual abuse history can remind us of, is the life of a seashell. Not knowing that there is beauty in what was 'left behind, to wash ashore and simply be.' God specifically spoke to me as I laid on the seashore, crying out to hear His voice. He gave me *Seashells* to remind you that you were never chosen to simply wash ashore and be overlooked or feel bad for all that has happened to you. You are so much more, and He CHOSE YOU to have life for His unique and sometimes mysterious glory!

Prayer

God, Your daughter sometimes feels useless, yet an ornament of beauty. God I am asking that You fill her with purpose, with Your love, with Your tenderness. I am asking that You show her even though she may not feel it now, that she was created to be more than the beautiful face that people often see. I love You and I thank you for the journey that she has endured in being hand selected by You.

Amen!

BEAUTIFUL

I cried today
I cried
Because He told me I was beautiful.

I cried today
I cried
Because it was the first time
I was able to look her in the eyes
And see beauty, flaws and all.

I cried today
I cried
Because I felt the fibers of self-doubt
Low self-esteem, release from my pores
To never return

I cried today
I cried
Because it felt great to smile back at her
My seemingly enemy

I cried today
I cried
Because for the first time
I saw me
His perfect masterpiece.

Scripture

Song Of Solomon 4:7 (NIV)

"You are altogether beautiful, my darling; there is no flaw in you."

Reflection

We often times think that our beauty has vanished when our abuse took place, to never reappear. But we know that God created us, in His image, to be beautiful not only to others, but to ourselves. As God whispers His sweet tunes in your ears today, know that you are beautiful to Him and dare to take a look in the mirror today and see His BEAUTIFUL masterpiece!

Prayer

Lord we thank You for this day. We honor You for creating us to be a beautiful gem. Please help my sister to see herself as You see her, a beautiful masterpiece. Lord, remove any pain from Your precious daughters' heart in regards to her beauty and her confidence. Give her the eyes to see your wonderful creation, her. With You, all things are made new. Glory to Your name!

Amen!

SMILES & STYLE

I smile
You say "You're so pretty!"
I style
You say, "You look beautiful!"
It's like I'm in a photo shoot
Waiting for the creative director
To give me my next move.

But the only difference is
This is reality
And you don't know
What's behind that smile & style.

I smile & style
To hid the pain.
I smile & style
To hid low self-esteem.
I smile & style
To trick you into believing
I have it all together
But I'm a wreck
Ridiculously unfastened.

You would think I'll be rotten
Like week old food
But One thing has kept me preserved
God.

He opened my eyes to see
Why I chose to smile & style
And feel good on the inside
So now when you see me
I glow
Because the Son is showing.

Scripture

Philippians 1:6 (NLT)

"And I am certain that God, who began the good work within you, will continue His work until it is finally finished on the day when Christ Jesus returns."

Reflection

I'm guilty. Guilty of tricking people into believing I'm ok everyday of my life by wearing beautiful clothes, a bad pair of shoes and luminous smile. SIKE! I was so broken and all of those wonderful compliments did nothing for the gaping hole that was on the inside of me. Not until I truly established a relationship with God did I begin to appreciate my smile and ridiculously high heels. It took God actually healing my hurt, pain, anger, unforgiveness, torments, jealously and so much more for me to appreciate the woman that I am. He is the only One who can make you whole, not a fake smile or a beautiful leather clutch. ONLY Him! But I would be remised to say, when He completely heals your soul, throwing on those diamonds, a bad pair of heels and your beautiful smile will only cause the Son to shine through you that much more!

Prayer

Father, Your daughter is beautiful and I am asking that You give her healing in her inner being Lord. There is nothing that can take the place of Your healing and Your love in our lives. I am asking that You replace the "things" that have been taking Your space in my sister's life, with You. Keep Your promises on her heart to encourage her to seek You in all things Lord. You have a work to complete in Your daughter and this pathway to healing will activate all the parts of her purpose to align. I love You and ask that you continue to teach her to trust You. In Jesus' name.

Amen!

DIAMOND

I see you,
Shining like the most coveted treasure,
A woman desires,
A diamond worth infinite amounts.

I see you,
Bursting at the seams
With such class and demure.

I see you,
Glowing like the rays of light,
Bouncing off of a mirror,
Blinding to whoever looks.

I see you,
Commanding the room,
With your luminous smile,
You're everything and more.

I see you,
Rocking the tales of truth,
That your Father created you
To be flawless and bright too.
I love who you are,
All the way through.

Remember that Daddy loves
EVERY part of you!

Scripture

Matthew 5:16 (KJV)

"Let your light so shine before men, that they may see your good works, and glorify your Father which is in heaven."

Reflection

It's something about a woman who commands the room. Commands the room with style, class, grace, but most importantly, God living in her. I envision that woman as you. You may have never dreamed of her being you or thought of yourself as being "that woman" everyone admires. But it is you. That woman is you because you live a life that has been built out of ashes and pressure. The most coveted jewel, a diamond, comes from the muck and the mire of ashes and pressure. A diamond shines like it is supposed to once it is pulled out of a dark and dreary place. Believe that you deserve to shine just like a diamond at this juncture in your life. You have been pulled out of the muck and mire and you have been polished to shine!

Prayer

Letting Your light shine through me Father is the most honorable thing I can do for You. For I have lived the life of fear, pain, shame and many other adjectives that I can think of but once I invited You to live in me, all of those negative chains of my past were broken. I thank You for the opportunity to be a living vessel for others to see what You can do with broken pieces. I humble myself as You continue to show me who I am through You. In Your Son's name I pray.

Amen!

ME

I don't see me
I see straight through
When I look in the mirror.

Hair on point
Panty lines don't show
Makeup flawless.

But I hate the woman
Who creates the shadows
That are filled with nothing.

What made me see
Nothing but strands
Of useless pieces you ask?

I don't know,
I guess I can say
I've always felt this way.

Just a woman with curves and a voice
As someone takes me for a test drive,
While my gas tank is on E.

I got tired of being nothing one day
And prayed an earnest prayer.

Lord, will you renew my spirit and the fibers of me?
I have never felt joy or a smile in my soul.
I know I have only been here
For as long as it took you to begin your ministry
But I know not who I am or what it is to be me.
Show me everything it takes to be beautiful
Smart and living for you.
Shameful it is
But I trust that as I live my days
You will give me the joy I need to laugh and feel free.

Scripture

Psalm 139:14 (ESV)

"I praise you, for I am fearfully and wonderfully made. Wonderful are your works; my soul knows it very well."

Reflection

How many times have you heard yourself say, "You're nothing!" "You're too fat!" "You're not pretty!" I can say I felt the exact same way. I had no idea how I was going to get out of that dark hole, I just couldn't see my way out. I was tired of hearing negative talk about who God created me to be in my own head. As I began to get tired of hearing such negativity over and over again, God revealed to me, I was speaking against His creation. I asked for a way to see myself how He sees me and He gave me a formula. Speak positive words over my life every time I heard a negative thought. When I first began this exercise, it seemed a little fake because I was used to hearing false truths. But as I continued to feed myself positive fruit, I began to believe it and so did everyone else! God is not in the game of tricking you into believing you are perfectly made for Him. It is His desire for you to believe in you so you can live how He wired you to live for His Kingdom.

Prayer

If my sister is filled with negative self-affirmations Lord, please show her who she is, just the way You see her. I honor you for being so thoughtful about her uniqueness and the purpose that you have placed in her. Help her to see a new part of her everyday, inside and out, that is beautiful and special to you. Thank you for removing the blinders and the damaging thoughts and behaviors that is keeping her separated from seeing the pure essence of her beauty. We honor you for being so thoughtful. We ask these things in Jesus' name.

Amen!

BEAUTY ACTIVITY

According to *Dove Research: The Real Truth About Beauty: Revisited*, only 4% of women around the world consider themselves beautiful (up from 2% in 2004). In all honesty, 100% of women around the world should consider themselves beautiful. According to Genesis 1:27 (NLV), "And God made man in His own likeness. In the likeness of God He made him. He made both male and female." How could you not feel beautiful knowing you were made in the image of God? It's sort of a blow to God to create you with such individuality, yet still in His image and deny who you are.

The fact is, women who don't feel beautiful is exacerbated by a shameful and ugly act of sexual abuse. There is no way the enemy thought you would ever arise from the ashes of your pain, but God knew and saw different when He created you. You are not junk, you were made with order and a purpose. Beauty is not for those we see everyday on television or in magazines. Beauty is for every person living, and that includes you!

BEAUTY ACTIVITY

In today's exercise, we will discover who we are in God's eyes. Taking time to fully know what God says about us is important. It gives us a unique and personal perspective that the world does not show us.

For this exercise you will need the following:

1. Washcloth
2. Facial Soap
3. Water
4. Mirror

INSTRUCTIONS

1. Wash your face with your facial soap removing all makeup.
2. Dry your face clean.
3. Stand in front of your mirror and look at every inch of you, staying free of negative thoughts and comments.
4. Smile.
5. Look at yourself in the eyes for 10 seconds.
6. What do you see? Only use "I am" statements such as, "I am pretty". Remember, positive statements only!
7. Write down everything you say you are.
8. If you were not able to come up with any positive phrases, here are a few for you to recite:
    - I am a unique child of God, the Creator of all things
    - I am beautiful and smart
    - I am confident
    - I am embracing who I am
    - I am letting go of my fears of being beautiful
    - I am happy in my own skin
    - I am a beautiful gift to my family, friends, church, and community
    - I am free from the judgment of others, including myself

TIME WITH GOD

Often times we look to the world to show and teach us how to be beautiful. In actuality, we can only turn to our Father to approve and show us our inner and outer beauty. During today's prayer and fasting time with God (please read page ii for fasting guidance), rest every doubt about your sense of beauty with Him:

1. Read Psalm 139:14.

2. Pray and ask God to reveal to you in His Word the areas in which you are beautiful and are uniquely made to His image. Reveal your true feelings about your ability to see yourself as a beautiful woman. Give every harmful thought or action that negates your beauty over to God to emancipate your mind and spirit from believing you are beautiful.

3. Fast and meditate on your time spent with God today.

LOVE & RELATIONSHIPS

IT'S NOT SUBJECTIVE

Tenderness and love
It's what we all desire
As we grow into delicate flowers
Trimmed and groomed by our loved ones.
Backs are turned to tender other precious pedals
And my pedals are plucked.

My love begins to run low.

Fears to be snapped at the vine
And taken out by the familiar
I break in the very place I feared.
My supply of love to feed me daily
Has stopped instantly
I am now wilted and dusty.

My groomer is so distraught
Over the brokenness she sees
She begins to cry
And remembers her own broken vines.

A Specialist came in town
Because He heard my groomer's cries to quit
He came to teach me how to grow
In all kinds of weather.

"I simply have to know
How to grow and feed myself
I can't keep up like this."
I say while talking to my Specialist.

I felt a shift.
A shift in who I know myself to be
My groomer has never
Made me feel like this
It had to be He.

It is now obvious
My life does not depend on who is grooming
Or cutting me deep
I can only live and love
For the One who created me.

Scripture

John 13:34 (NIV)

"A new command I give you: Love one another. As I have loved you, so you must love one another."

Reflection

I confronted my abuser. I made the decision to do so as I wrote this devotional. God impressed it upon me to take that step. I was afraid and I was fearful of how it would all play out. I prayed for God to lead me and give me peace in his presence, and He did. I have never felt such peace around my abuser, I was always on edge. In the process of the confrontation, one thing remained constant, my love for him. I saw him through the eyes of Christ. I shared with him how God has healed my brokenness and it is only through Him I have been made whole. I saw the moment the Holy Spirit spoke to him as I looked him in the eyes and smiled, because I know he heard His voice. As I left his home, a friend reminded me, "You hugged him!" If I am honest, it was the love of God that worked through me. Never would I have imagined I would have such peace and love for someone who tore my life apart from a young age. God used me so my abuser could see Him in the flesh. Love is not subjective, It knows no boundaries.

Prayer

Lord, I thank You for showing us what true love is, it has no boundaries, no filter, no edge, but only has the Truth. I ask right now that You show Your daughter what Your unconditional love looks like, the love of Christ. Descend upon her now as You shift her view of a love that only You can give, as she witnesses to people with her story. We love You and thank You. In Jesus' name.

Amen!

NIGHTLIGHT

The moon shines
And caresses my skin
As we walk hand and hand on the boardwalk.
Taken aback by the essence of natures beauty
You lean in for a kiss.

Struck by emotions
I don't know how to control
I allow you to lead me home
Where our encounters are daily
Behind four walls.

If they could talk
They would tell the tales of my tail
Exposed for the love of another
Who is not my husband
But a shadow
Creeping by my hallway nightlight
That illuminates the pathway towards the exit.

My door closes with such strength
That leaves me every time
My treasure box is opened to a foreigner
Who did not belong in my home.

My nightlight is still illuminated
In hopes that the love
I have to give is exposed
And picked up by someone
Who can simply understand
I choose to love this way
Because I have not allowed my Father
To completely heal me.

Scripture

1 Corinthians 6:19-20 (NLT)

"Don't you realize that your body is a temple of the Holy Spirit, who lives in you and was given to you by God? You do not belong to yourself, for God bought you with a high price. So you must honor God with your body."

Reflection

Love is not late night visits. Love is not dinner and a movie and a ride back to your place, unmarried. Love is not dependent upon how many times you wash your sheets. Love is not you getting the latest shoes or weave so you can be someone's fantasy. Love as a survivor can be extremely delicate and very intricate. All of these 'things' lit up my world when a man would 'treat me like a lady.' The definition of love comes from Christ himself, a Gentleman who will never press you to accept who He is but will pursue you with everything He has simply to show you His respect and love, which is unconditional and not contingent upon what you can give Him. The truth is, we all desire love and affection, respect and adoration, but no one, and I mean no one, can give you this BEFORE you have it for yourself. In order to recognize and appreciate it in someone else, you have to know what it looks like for yourself. You are the most important person in your sphere of influence. Take care of you first.

Prayer

Father, only You know the intentions and agendas of people we are in relationship with. I ask You to expose their intentions on our behalf. I also ask You to give Your daughter the ability to love herself and see her worth, just as You see her Lord. I trust that You will give her a new pair of eyes to see herself as a new creature, washed in Your blood and full of beauty and worth. Give her a renewed mind to remember Your Word in relation to her existence and Your promises for her future life in love. In Jesus' name.

Amen!

I LOVE HIM, I DO!

"Shut the hell up!"
You have no idea
How worse my mouth gets
No one will ever know
I just slapped you in my mind
It's not all that bad
My attitude towards others…
I have a burden
That's bigger than me
I deserve to be pissed.

'Love' shown in the middle of the night
While everyone is sleep
Many ask
"Why are you so angry?"
They see me!
I'm exposed
I thought I was hiding everything so well.
Snapping back, I lie and say
"I'm just tired…"
When on the inside
I'm full of grief
I deserve to be pissed.

To church I go
Every Sunday
I can't miss out
On the Lord blessing me
The Pastor preached love,
Unconditionally.
A sudden flash
So many people look up to me
Anger & frustration
You must go.

The Lord & I have
A bond no one can see
Expressing His love
Makes me uncomfortable
It means I'll have to let go
Of all that has been built around me
Walls to protect my heart
To keep me safe from others.

I look to you Lord
For guidance on how to be
More loving, and less of my history.

Scripture

Ephesians 5:4 (NIV)

"Nor should there be obscenity, foolish talk or coarse joking, which are out of place, but rather thanksgiving."

Reflection

I remember throughout my life people would say I was mean and cold. I would get angry when people told me this because I knew I was a loving woman on the inside. So what was it that had me hurting everyone's feelings or cutting them off because they were 'weird'. I would have to say my inability to realize God's love for me. I didn't understand He loved me because I was someone who was abused and did so many wrong things. I would often think, "I am nothing, how can He love me?" I did not understand why He could love someone as washed up as me, so I began to actually act that out. I was mean and nasty to others because I didn't know how to receive love or much less be love. And it hit me one day, the pain, sorrow, nightmares, broken relationships, all of it will be able to help someone. But no one will believe God is a healer or a provider if I keep this defensive behavior up. I had to pray constantly that God would show me how I was being angry and nasty to others, for no fault of their own, and replace it with His love, grace and peace. This is a continued prayer of mine. Others are watching how we walk our healing out. Will you continue to use the excuse of your abuse taking place to not show the love of God? He is mighty to save and can change your behaviors, you just have to trust Him.

Prayer

God, we know that Your love is perfect and our love is flawed. But I am asking You in the name of Jesus, You break all negative behaviors in Your daughter that is not showing Your love. We are a light to shine amongst Your people and may Your glory shine through Your daughter Lord. Remove all defensive actions and attitudes in the name of Jesus. Replace it with love, gentleness, kindness and hope. In Jesus' Name.

Amen!

FRIENDSHIPS

I never really liked people
They always scared me
I was given the opportunity
To date millionaires
To be amongst the elite
To be amongst the "lowly"
And I never fit in.
I fit in
In my own world
On my couch
In my kitchen
Alone.

I never really liked people
We always laughed together, publically
On trips
At theme parks
At church
But I never fit in.
I did fit in
In my home
On my couch
In my kitchen
Alone.

I've always loved people
It's what recharged me
And let's me see another side of life
Culture, opinions, laughter, fun and most importantly, support.
You see, I have this thing that I have tired to keep under wraps for years
But it creeps up every time I meet someone new
It happened so long ago
But the thought of someone else getting close to me, is scary.

I've always loved people
It's what God created us for
To be in relationship
Male or female
It's a joyous thing
But I can't help to think
If hurt will knock on my doorstep yet again.

Scripture

John 15:12 (NLT)

"This is my commandment: Love each other in the same way I have loved you."

Reflection

Establishing friendships can be hard as a survivor. You feel awkward, you feel out of place, and you feel empty at the same time. Or maybe establishing friendships are super easy and you are the life of the party, you feel like you fit right in, and you still feel empty inside. Trust has been broken as a survivor and creating a healthy friendship, with boundaries that are mutually beneficial, is not hard with the help of our Savior! Say this prayer as a way to reassure yourself, He is able.

Prayer

Lord, I want healthy friendships that edify my spirit. Friendships that are mutually beneficial and free from fear, timidity, false representation, and full of trust. I know that with Your discernment, You will cultivate awesome relationships that are supportive of who I am and my *Pathways to Healing*. I praise You, In Jesus' Name.

Amen!

HUNGRY

1 Peter 5:6-7
1 John 4:7-8
Psalm 86:15
Proverbs 8:17
Psalm 136:26
Colossians 2:6-7
Romans 5:8
Lamentations 3:22-23
Zephaniah 3:17
Proverbs 10:12
Romans 8:37-39
Colossians 3:14
Psalm 18:1

I'm full.

Scripture

John 3:16 (NLT)

"For God so loved the world: He gave his one and only Son, so that everyone who believes in him will not perish but have eternal life."

Reflection

I don't know anyone who can out give God, especially in love. I have read books, gotten advice from friends, even seen others display love, but nothing and no one explains and demonstrates love better than God Himself. Love can be mystifying, especially as a survivor. We have various levels of love, which are typically compartmentalized primarily because of fear and rejection. I think to the day Christ decided to give His life for us, it was the most loving day in history. No man or woman could have ever thought that living and dying in the name of saving thousands of generations of people, would be the single most important act of love in the history of mankind. No you cannot ever give of yourself what Christ gave of Himself for you. But I challenge you to understand the magnitude of endurance, peace, clarity, and most importantly love, it took for Him to stand in the gap for you and me. Tap into that love and watch Him begin to release hardened pieces from around your heart.

Prayer

Lord, it gets tough when we think about love and allowing others into a vulnerable place of our being. I ask now that You diligently take our hand as we learn to love others, as You have commanded us. Set us free from the traps of experiencing the best thing that can ever happen to us, Your love. I ask that You protect us from the wolves who circle around us to take advantage of us in vulnerable times. I ask all of these things in Your Son's precious name.

Amen!

LOVE & RELATIONSHIP ACTIVITY

Love and relationships are the basis of our existence. We all desire to be loved, nurtured and the center of someone's life. There are different types of relationships that yield different types of love such as familial relationships, friend and associate relationships, romantic relationships, professional relationships and the list goes on. Actually, I missed the most important relationship we will ever establish, a relationship with God. I never knew while growing up that this would be my most important relationship. Knowing God made my life have meaning in the darkest times. The best part of our relationship is I don't have to beg Him to rescue me, He already desires to.

In our relationship with God, we have boundaries that He has established for us which will bring Him honor but most importantly show that we love Him. Reading Exodus 20:1-17, God clearly states His boundaries for us, the ten commandments. I thought about why we are called to love people, especially those who are a menace to our lives. It is clear, without love, those who have come against us, will not be able to see Christ. Often times we will feel like we do not have a voice to speak up for ourselves or a choice in a particular matter. But we have the perfect example of what a relationship is like with healthy boundaries, love and trust.

In the *Trust* chapter, we established the foundation of what it takes to sustain a relationship, trust. We will take it a step further and learn how to create healthy boundaries in those relationships, while valuing our self-worth.

LOVE & RELATIONSHIP ACTIVITY

In establishing relationships, we have to set healthy boundaries which are mutually exclusive. Without those healthy boundaries, we are bound to be used and continue to remain broken. Today we will learn how to exercise our ability to gain the respect we deserve and most importantly, value our worth.

1. **Where do you stand?** Analyze where you are emotionally, physically, mentally, and spiritually. Without a baseline of your tolerance level, you will not be able to establish healthy boundaries.
2. **What does my previous and current relationships say about me?** How we were raised, in addition to the effects of sexual abuse, really sets the tone of our present day characteristics. Examine the patterns you have noticed in your relationships and consider if you have been putting yourself last.
3. **How do you feel?** We tend to ignore red flags because they make us feel uncomfortable and baffled on how to address them. Red flags were created to protect us from boundaries that are not to be crossed, don't despise them.
4. **What are you not saying?** To ensure our boundaries are not crossed, we have to say what is making us feel uncomfortable. Being honest in your relationships yields mutually beneficial results. Without being honest, you will continually feel as though you are given left overs in your relationships. Speak up!
5. **How are things going?** Considering yourself in a relationship shows the value of who you are. It also illustrates that you have the ability to exercise control over a situation. Take the time to reflect on your feelings and interactions to ensure you are considering healthy choices for your well-being and also to discover how you can work through similar interactions in the future.
6. **How am I taking care of myself?** Your ability to honor how you feel in relationships is a key indicator of whether or not you are genuinely taking care of you. If you feel yourself slipping in your boundaries and constantly compromising to another's benefit, you are not taking care of yourself. Be true to your boundaries and voice!
7. **Am I following through?** Your boundaries have been set and it is now your opportunity to follow through with ensuring that those boundaries are not crossed. Take the time to respectfully convey your boundary.
8. **Am I taking on too much?** It takes time to build healthy relationships, try not to implement too many boundaries at one time. Managing and implementing a few boundaries at a time will allow you to practice and develop your boundaries and strengthen your voice.
9. **Who is in my corner?** Always remember you have a support team on your side! Call those who are walking with you on this journey, friends, family, therapist, etc. Practice your boundaries together to build your confidence and clearly develop your voice.

TIME WITH GOD

Loving others past our place of comfort is rough. But the great thing about having Christ in our lives is He gives us the perfect example of what it means to love. Developing loving relationships that speak to the very essence of who we are as people is the goal of creating a healthy relationship. Through practice, healthy relationships will begin to feed you in ways you never thought possible, it's very rewarding to say you have a positive relationship with a loved one. But one relationship in particular matters the most, the relationship with our Father. Today we will take time to not only pray and fast about our relationship with people (please read page ii for fasting guidance), but our relationship with God:

1. Read Psalm 63:1-8.

2. Pray about your ability to reverently be in a relationship with God so He can live and speak through you. Pray that through your relationship with Him, you are able to gain wisdom and insight on how to love yourself and others and your ability to create healthy boundaries with those you are in relationship with.

3. Fast and meditate on your time spent with God today.

GRACE

TOP OF THE MORNING

I always keep up
In everything I do
Work, college, bills
Ok, let me stop
I messed up a time or two.

Choosing to be perfect
Is all I knew
Keeping my life stitched together
Is the only option I have to live.

If I keep in line
I have control
Over my life
And no one will know.

The abuse, lies, tricks, and vices
I've had to brave
It gives me the license
To create my own life
Pretty and in sync.

But the truth is
I don't know what to think.

I've come to the end of my rope
With everything I do
To deliver a façade
That is melting away
Like ice cream in the sun
I just know there is hope.

To live a life free of false joy
Because I can no longer keep this pace
Lord show me this thing I keep hearing about,
The wonderful place of grace.

Scripture

Hebrews 4:16 (NLT)

"So let us come boldly to the throne of our gracious God. Then we will receive his mercy, and we will find his grace to help us when we need it most."

Reflection

You have a choice, to pressure your life to be perfect since you didn't have control over your abuse. Or you can let God do His job all by Himself by giving you grace. As a believer, we are taught faith. Increase your faith and it will increase your healing. Increase your faith and it will increase your peace. Actually, this is a little backwards. We do need faith as believers to activate grace that is on our lives. What is grace? In Webster's Dictionary and in Scripture (Ezra 9:8), grace has been defined as **God's unmerited favor towards man**. The beauty of grace is that you cannot earn it, all you have to do it accept it. Have you realized that the grace of God has been on your life until this very day? His grace was revealed to me when I was finally able to tell someone about my abuse. His grace became real to me as a teenager and young adult when I became sexually active and engaged in risky behaviors. But God! God's grace is sufficient for your life when you acknowledge the checklist of things you do to make your life livable can be handled by God himself. Allow God to exercise His grace in your life. All He needs you to do is have the faith, which will activate His grace!

Prayer

Father, You know the difficulties Your daughter faces everyday as she embarks upon fixing her life on her own. Lord, give her the clear understanding of what it means to accept the grace You freely give to heal her mind, body, and spirit. I trust You are full of grace and will support her efforts of believing and trusting in You. In Jesus' name.

Amen!

HE IS TEACHING ME

Trust by far is not my cup of tea
But from looking over my life,
He sure is teaching me.

Ways to take hold of my future with Him
Sometimes it's a struggle,
But I know I will win.

I remember sitting and taking a breath
Telling Him,
"Lord, I have nothing left."

Empty, yet full of such waste
He decided to show His hands,
Full of grace.

I can enter at my leisure
And leave all my belongings behind,
Without fear of being judged.

In this place called grace
I have a peace of mind
It's a mysterious concept,
For a woman like me.

To trouble God
I'll be a fool to think,
His grace isn't sufficient enough.

All my troubles are gone in a blink
I love Him,
I never thought I'd be so free.

He is faithful and true to character
That He has no problem,
With softly teaching me.

Scripture

Romans 3:24 (ESV)

"And are justified by His grace as a gift, through the redemption that is in Christ Jesus."

Reflection

The grace of God was unheard of while I was growing up in church. It was more so along the lines of, "the grace of God was on your life when you slept with that John that night and you didn't get AIDS." A portion of this statement is true. The portion of this statement that is true is, "you didn't get AIDS" but it is not the grace of God that saved one from contracting AIDS, it's the mercy of God that saved one from contracting AIDS. Grace and mercy often get mixed up, it's the blood of Jesus that keeps us from receiving punishment for our sins, while grace is given to us to help us navigate through life. Grace always seemed as though it was a mystical thing that hung out in outer space and was zapped to me only when I was in dangerous situations. This couldn't be farther from the truth. Grace can be given when you are on your job and you need peace and clarity to complete a project that you know nothing about. Grace can be given to you when you have unknowingly sinned and you can't seem to forgive yourself. We miss the mark at times with accepting God's unmerited grace because it seems so unnatural to not be condemned for something that was wrong. But by accepting grace, you acknowledge, 'I am nothing without You, but with You I am everything.' It's hard to conceive that something is given to us without working for it. That's the beauty of Christ, grace is a free gift He gives us, which will change our lives.

Prayer

God we loose sight sometimes of what really matters in life and often times we need You to pick us up and teach us. We open our hearts to You right now to what it means to accept the gift of grace. To free our lives of chaos and accept the peace that comes from living in Your grace. Teach us the will of Your ways as we accept Your great grace on our *Pathways to Healing*. It's in Your Son's name we pray.

Amen!

I'LL TAKE IT!

Shoes, clothes, vacations, money
Make me feel great when I initially purchase.
Stepping in my Target shoes
While smoothing out my latest thrift store find.
I smile because I look like a few hundred bucks
But money has been kept in my pocket
Which are really empty because of the 'blessing' I just parked.

God has shown me favor when it comes to these things
But I often wonder
If these things went up in flames tomorrow
Would I have anything left?
Would my hard earned money go back into replacing my goods?

"Grace, you should choose."

He spoke clear as my Android would say
Thoughts began to rush my psyche
Never would I embrace the truth
If I hadn't heard His voice.

Nothing replaced Your vision and mission for me
Your grace is for me to carry through life.
I misused it on a pair of shoes
But You are still gracious
All you do is gently show me You.

Scripture

John 1:16 (NLT)

"From his abundance we have all received one gracious blessing after another."

Reflection

How many times have we said it was the grace of God that let me see the paper to the department store that was having a sale on a pair of shoes you have been wanting? I'll raise my hand! I confused my mismanagement or over spending the blessing He has given me, via my job, as favor and grace. But God is so gracious, He carries us through our hard and our 'ignorance is bliss' times with still being blessed! He taught me a lesson, to take the grace He is giving me in those mismanagement times and apply is to the areas in which He expects me to produce in, working for the Kingdom. Grace is not an excuse to continue on the path we have been walking, but the opportunity to acknowledge our mistakes and make corrections in the future.

Prayer

God, Your love for us is so powerful, while we are still in out mess, You extend us grace as we wake up to You. we honor You for being the perfect example of what it means to live endlessly. It is Your grace that carries us everyday and we pray that You would align our priorities to further Your agenda of growing the Kingdom. In Jesus' name.

Amen!

LEAN ON ME

Birds chirping
Buses passing by
Tears flowing
My spirit is full of hope
Yet I have nothing left in me to give.

I choose to live
For a God I have never seen
But felt and heard
My capacity to make my life work
Is nothing I want to do.

Laid in a puddle of tears
I turn my head
He whispers to me,
"I have all the grace
You will ever need."

I'm too drained
My only response is to blink.

I close my eyes
And He sweeps me up in a vision.
It's time to keep watch
Of His precious children.

I open my eyes
And He left me be
"God, I have nothing left to give."
He says, " Sweet pea, just lean on Me."

Scripture

Isaiah 40:29 (NLT)

"He gives power to the weak and strength to the powerless."

Reflection

I felt empty. Like my life and everyone in it was too much. Bills, friends, trips, family, work, projects, and last but not least me working on healing a very broken. It was just too much. I can't do it all. As a matter of fact, I couldn't do anything at all. I have to leave it ALL in God's hands for Him to move according to His will for my benefit. Have you ever heard the saying, "Do what you can and leave the rest to God?" I particularity do not like that phrase, it gives the false reality that we have the power to do most of the things we can do in our lives and then when we can't figure the rest out, we give God our left overs to sort through. That is such an insult to Him. He desires to be our everything in every situation. I say, "Give God everything and wait for instruction." God is here to fix every minuet aspect of our lives, even the things we don't think about. You are NOT superwoman. Accept God's grace to rest in Him and trust Him to move on your behalf.

Prayer

Thank You Lord for always being there for us. Even when we don't think we need You. We accept the grace to rest in You and allow You to be the God of our lives. Take over in our households, our marriages, our finances, our emotions, and most importantly, our healing. We trust there is no god like You who cares about our smallest request. We thank You now for the opportunity to rest on You for every detail of our lives. In Jesus' name.

Amen!

JUST ONE THING

I toil and smile
Trying to realize
There is only one thing
That will make You happy.

The innocence of a child
Running to You
With such joy
Everyday.

I keep You in the small of my heart
There is nothing like
The kisses of your own
After a long days work.

"Yes Daddy" and "Yes Sir"
Shows my respect to You
There is only one thing that matters
Amongst so many others
And that's simply,
Living my life for You.

Scripture

Matthew 6:33 (NLT)

"Seek the Kingdom of God above all else, and live righteously, and he will give you everything you need."

Reflection

We make life complicated at times and I am so guilty of this. We figure out our career paths, our financial paths, our retirement paths, our traveling paths, and so many other paths, that we forget the number one path we are to journey upon. The path to Christ. We are to live our lives with such dedication and admiration to Christ in every path we travel in life, there should be no question of our direction. It is so much easier to have a tangible 'rewarding' path as our focus from day to day. But our true and only path is the path to Christ, it's what will keep our lives free from pain and overflowing in blessings.

Prayer

This walk seems so unrewarding at times Lord. Sometimes we don't know who or where to go, or who to be, but there is so much You have in store for us. Reveal it to us Father. I am asking You right now, in the name of Jesus, to remind us daily of Your number one purpose for our lives, to live for You. Keep us safe as we cross paths with familiar and unfamiliar spirits that may deter us from living for You. Thank You in advance for the courage to be Your living vessel. In Jesus' name.

Amen!

GRACE ACTIVITY

There is not a time that goes by that your Father does not want to extend His grace towards you. Day in and day out we fight with the ability to 'be a Christian' or 'forgive others' because for so long we were taught rules and regulations that if we failed to follow, we were not pleasing God. Yet it is through grace we are saved, prosper, obey and live. In 2 Peter 1:2-3 (NIV), Peter writes, "Grace and peace be yours in abundance through the knowledge of God and of Jesus our Lord. His divine power has given us everything we need for a godly life through the knowledge of him who called us by his own glory and goodness."

It is through grace we are saved by the blood of The Lamb. It is through grace we receive our blessings from God. It is through grace we will have the heart to obey and follow God. It is through grace we live life the way God intended us to live. It is only through grace you can continue on your *Pathways to Healing*. You have been given access to the Kingdom to LIVE as a survivor through God's divine power of grace.

GRACE ACTIVITY

In today's activity, we will have a bit of reciting and exercise, but I am sure you will be able to fully understand the grace of our loving God once we are done. Before getting to our activity, picture something that is low in cost, $10.00 or less, that would be a reward or treat to you. Got it in your mind? Ok great. Let's get started!

For this exercise complete the following in 30 seconds or less. Once you complete our activity today in the specified timeframe, head out and buy your treat as a reward for doing a great job. Ready? Set. GO!

1. 50 jumping jacks
2. Call a friend and tell them you love them
3. Recite the books of the Bible backwards

Did you finish in time? Take some time to read 1 Timothy 1:12-17.

It was absolutely impossible to complete today's activity right? There is no way you could have done all of that in 30 seconds! But so often we pressure ourselves to be perfect and when we fail these unrealistic goals, we beat ourselves up. Just the same way, it is humanly impossible to live up to the standards that God has outlined in His Word. But it is only through His grace, He extended us mercy (Romans 6:23) so we don't have to pay for our shortcomings because the Father sent Jesus to pay for every last one of them. Now that you understand our Father's love, grace and mercy, be gracious to yourself and still go out and buy your treat! After all, even when you fall short, it's what your Father would do.

TIME WITH GOD

Grace is the covering you want to live under forever. There is nothing you or anyone else can do take to it away from you. But it is easy to ignore if you don't understand its power. As we spend much needed time with our Father today praying and fasting (please read page ii for fasting guidance), remember the grace and mercy God extended to you long ago, is still waiting to be opened and utilized, so you can walk in freedom and love on your *Pathways to Healing*:

1. Read Romans 3:20-24.

2. Pray and ask God to show you areas in your life where you need to accept His grace. Ask Him to give you a renewed mind when it comes to recognizing His grace and extending that same grace to others.

3. Fast and meditate on your time spent with God today.

Our journey through *Pathways to Healing* has come to an end. There have been highs and there have been lows as you have walked towards healing. I pray that in the next coming days, months and years, revelation is given to you about this journey you have taken. As this life long journey continues, always remember you have someone praying for you, you are stronger than you think and your Father is guiding you.

Thank you for trusting me to carry you through this journey. Until next time, be beautiful!

Kimberly R. Mayes, MSW

REFERENCES

D'Agostino, H., Etcoff, N., Orbach, S., & Scott, J. (2004) "The Real Truth About Beauty: A Global Report. Findings of the Global Study on Women, Beauty and Well-Being." *Dove Research*, *4*, 1-48.

Merriam-Webster Dictionary 2013

Spiritual Gifts Questionnaire: www.gifts.churchgrowth.org

www.ingramcontent.com/pod-product-compliance
Lightning Source LLC
Chambersburg PA
CBHW032055090426
42744CB00005B/224